P9-EFJ-942

CONTENTS

ACKNOWLEDGEMENTS

This book is largely the result of experience and knowledge gained as the Manager of International Teams during the last nine years. My first acknowledgement therefore is to all those players who have played for the England Amateur Team or the Great Britain Olympic Team under my management, and who have worked so hard both in matches and in training, to develop my ideas on tactics and teamwork.

I am also grateful to Allen Wade, not only for reading the manuscript, but also for the many stimulating discussions we have had together on football tactics.

To Mrs. Inman who typed the whole of the manuscript I wish to record a special note of thanks and appreciation for her excellent work.

Last, and perhaps most of all, I wish to thank Sir Alfred Ramsey. I have greatly benefited from his advice, his suggestions and his encouragement.

FOREWORD

by The Author

This book is written from a background of nine years experience of coaching and managing the England Amateur International Team and the Great Britain Olympic Team. During these years I have found myself frequently in the position of managing a team which is playing against players who are technically far superior. I quickly came to terms with the fact that England's only chance of winning these matches lay in sound teamwork based on sound tactics. So it is for this reason that I have now written this book to give others the benefit of what I now know.

In conjunction with the writing of this book I have produced eleven films on the title subjects of chapters two to twelve namely:

1. Why goals are scored.
2. Pressurising.
3. Key factors in defensive play.
4. Creating space.
5. Support in attack.
6. Attacking opponents with and without the ball.
7. The do's and don'ts of passing.
8. Shooting.
9. Defending at set plays.
10. Attacking at set plays.
11. Goalkeeping.

I have found that in the teaching, and therefore the learning process, films can play a most vital part. I hope, therefore, that those whose task it is to coach and teach football will use this book in conjunction with the films.

I hope too that the reading of the book and the viewing of the films will prove enjoyable in itself. Association football has become a World game because it is so enjoyable to players and spectators alike. It is my submission that one will enjoy any game more if one can play it better, and appreciate any game more if one understands it more fully.

TACTICS AND TEAMWORK

CHAPTER 1

SYSTEMS OF PLAY

The importance of systems of play is exaggerated. It should be understood at the outset that there is no system which will overcome inaccurate passing or inaccurate shooting: there is no system which caters for players who will not support each other and there is no system which caters for players who will not or who cannot run.

Systems of play are concerned with the arrangement of the players on the field of play. The number of permutations of these players, however, really is quite small. Most Managers and Coaches would be agreed that one arranges the players in three groups :—

(a) Back players.
(b) Mid-field players.
(c) Forward players.

Most would agree also that four players are required at the back, not fewer than two players in the mid-field and not fewer than two players in forward positions—total agreement on eight players ! One is, therefore, left with two players to permutate as one wishes. It is possible to play both these players forward and the arrangement becomes 4-2-4. It is possible to play both these players in the mid-field and the arrangement becomes 4-4-2. It is possible to play one of the players in the mid-field and the other player forward and the arrangement becomes 4-3-3, or it is possible to play one of these players behind the back four players and the other one either in mid-field or forward and the arrangement becomes 1-4-3-2 or 1-4-2-3, all of which is very interesting but tells us remarkably little about systems of play.

The fact of the matter is that two teams can play with the same system, e.g. 4-3-3, and yet play in a completely different way. Why ? Because the players will be different and will be given different instructions. It is possible for one Manager to instruct his full-backs to look constantly for opportunities to move forward in advance of the ball. It is possible for the opposing Manager to instruct his full-backs never to move forward in advance of the ball. It is possible for one Manager to arrange his forward players to play with wingers and for the opposing Manager to arrange to play without wingers. The eventual pattern and arrangement will be very different.

England Captain Kevin Keegan meets Bulgaria's Ivkov before the match. A good captain must be a good tactician and a good leader. He is in every sense the representative of the manager on the field.

TACTICS AND TEAMWORK

When teams lose it is usually not because they played 4-3-3 instead of some other system, although a number of writers and commentators would have us believe that this is so. It is most frequently because the team failed to perform well one or more of the key factors in effective teamwork.

We do the spectator less than justice when we infer that the whole business of tactics is really systems of play. If the great mass of spectators is to enjoy football more, then we must help them to understand more and, therefore, appreciate more about the game.

All of us, Managers, Coaches, Writers and Commentators, should accept our share of blame for having introduced a certain confusion into Association Football. We have not worked hard enough at presenting the game in a simple easy-to-understand manner. There is little doubt that some have delighted in what they mistakenly believe to be cleverness. It has turned to confusion. Confusion for some players and most spectators. Cleverness, if only these people could realise it, involves being clear and simple.

As far as teams are concerned, Managers should understand that lack of clarity leads to lack of understanding and lack of understanding leads to lack of agreement and lack of agreement spells disunity and disaster.

However, back to systems. Modern systems really started in 1925 when the off-side law was changed. Before 1925 the law stated :—

A player is off-side if he is nearer his opponent's goal-line than the ball at the moment the ball is played unless :—

(a) He is in his own half of the field of play.

(b) There are *THREE* of his opponents nearer to their own goal-line than he is.

(c) The ball last touched an opponent or was played by him.

(d) He receives the ball direct from a goal-kick, a corner kick, a throw-in or when it was dropped by the referee.

All that happened in 1925 was to change one word in (b) to read :—

There are *TWO* of his opponents nearer to their own goal-line than he is.

The immediate result of the change was to make goals easier to score because attacking players could now score goals from positions where previously they would have been given off-side.

Effective system now required that more players were deployed at the back. That was duly done and the three full-back system emerged. There were, of course, lots of variations on a theme and there was certainly no shortage of words to describe the various

England manager, Ron Greenwood.

systems: but the basic tactical fact was that more players were now deployed in back positions.

There were some interesting tactical developments in the early 1950's but the next tactical landmark we must highlight was the World Cup of 1958 in which 126 goals were scored in 35 matches. This, of course, was the age of the 4-2-4 system of play. It was also the age of the Brazilians symbolising all that we thought best in attacking football. They showed us the way ahead . . . or did they?

In the World Cup of 1962, again won by the Brazilians, there were only 88 goals scored in 32 matches. Whatever happened to the golden age of attacking football and the 4-2-4? And how do we explain away 38 fewer goals—a decrease in goal productivity of approximately 25%. Another fact was that in 1962 Czechoslovakia, who were the runners up to Brazil, reached the semi-final after playing four matches and scoring three goals. Something had produced dividends and for the most part it was not attacking football. In simple terms more players were being deployed in back positions and fewer in forward positions. There was an emphasis too on deploying mid-field players with more thought on their defensive powers and less thought on their attacking ability. It was not uncommon to see eight or even nine players deployed in permanent or semi-permanent defensive positions. One needs, of course, very little imagination or tactical skill to deploy nine players in defence.

Had 1962 produced the end of the tactical road, the ultimate in tactical stalemate? Not a bit of it.

There was a problem and the problem was squarely at the feet of the Team Managers. But good Football Managers are not unlike good Generals—that which is known to succeed is retained, that which is known to fail is discarded. The issues upon which one is doubtful, one plays the percentages. By this we mean that one calculates on what will bring success most times. So one does not, upon calculating the percentages, encourage players to shoot from the half-way line.

That which succeeded in 1962, therefore, was going to be retained. Successful teams were going to defend with eight or nine players in withdrawn positions. The percentage chance of success, however, with only two forward players was very small. It was now evident that what was required were players who could withdraw into defence and also get forward to attack. There were three basic requirements.

(1) Players must have a high work-rate to undertake increased amounts of running and sustain their effort for 90 minutes.

(2) A greater understanding of how to play in various parts of the field. It became important, for example, for a full-back to understand how to play as a winger. There was little point in sending full-backs forward if they had no understanding of how to play in forward parts of the field.

(3) A greater range of techniques. Defensive players usually have a limited range of attacking techniques and their timing and weighting of passes is usually not as good as forward players. There was a need in 1962 to develop a greater range of techniques especially for the back players in attack. There was no merit, for example, in our full-backs knowing how to play as wingers if all the crosses went behind the goals for goal-kicks.

Fitness, understanding and technique are the three major ingredients in team performance. The less you have of one of those ingredients the more you must have of the other two.

The tactical position has now been reached where we can predict with certainty that no team will win a major championship without a high level of individual and team fitness. But fitness on its own is not enough. One requires also understanding. The importance of understanding can be explained in simple statistics. In a game of 90 minutes the ball is actually in play for approximately 60 minutes. For the remainder of the time the ball is out of play for goal-kicks, free kicks etc. Out of those 60 minutes, in an even game, each team will have approximately 30 minutes in possession of the ball and an individual player will have approximately three minutes in possession of the ball. For the remaining period of time he will work hard to make it as difficult as possible for his opponent to play effectively and he will work equally hard to make it easy for his team-mates to play effectively.

How a player makes this contribution as an individual and how the work of all individuals is organised into efficient team-work is very largely the subject of this book. Suffice it to say at this stage that Association Football is a game of decisions. It is a game where it is every bit as important to be a quick thinker as it is to be a quick mover. Quick thinking in football is not unlike quick thinking in anything else; it is the capacity for rapidly sifting the essential from the non-essential. In other words, understanding the key factors and knowing how and when to use them.

Technique obviously is important. It is important that all players should practise to increase their range of techniques. In competitive play, however, a player must come to terms with what he can do and concentrate upon doing it. A player too must learn to play the percentages, and if he cannot hit forty yard passes accurately

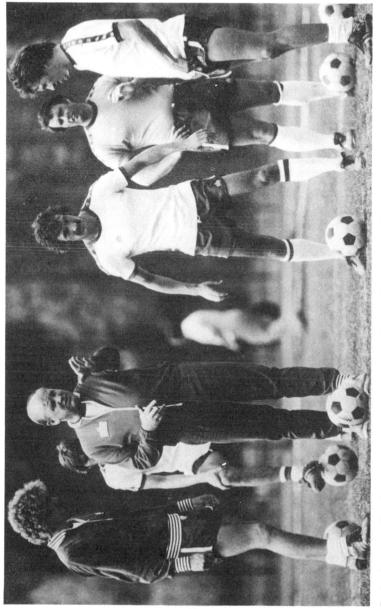

England manager Ron Greenwood makes a point during training in Vienna, June 1979.

his concentration should be on making the length of passes he can hit accurately.

There is little doubt that the game of the future will require players of greater technical ability in all positions, and one will be surprised if this is not one of the major characteristics of the World Cup in 1974. The development of greater technical ability without sacrificing work-rate will, however, be difficult to achieve. The challenge nevertheless is to improve technique without impairing the work-rate of the team.

There is little doubt either that the development of defensive techniques aimed at restricting both the time and the space in which an attacker has to play will continue. It is already evident that teams are becoming aware of the need to extract the maximum advantage from situations where the defence cannot force the player with the ball into error. These situations are set play situations, i.e. free-kick, corner and throw in. Not only is it possible to serve the ball in accurately from these situations but, of course, it is possible to send players forward who have special abilities, e.g. the heading of a tall centre half, and position these players in pre-planned areas. Teams will neglect the importance of set plays at their peril.

At the end of the day a Manager must decide on how he wants his team to play. He must select his players and he must arrange them to the best advantage. He will almost certainly have one or two pre-conceived ideas. For example, the full-backs must be quick, the centre-half must be a good header of the ball, one of the mid-field players must be a very good winner of the ball and of the forward players one must be able to pose a threat to the opposition in the air and so on. The Manager will then select and arrange his players to get the best out of them as individuals and the best out of them as a team. In doing this it is self-evident that the manner in which the team plays will represent their best chance of winning. If a Manager arranges and instructs his players with a view to getting the best out of them as individuals and as a team then that arrangement, that system is correct. The team may not win—it is not in mortals or Team Managers to command success; but they will have given themselves their best chance of winning. No one is entitled to ask for more, and no Manager should ever settle for less.

CHAPTER 2

WHY GOALS ARE SCORED

Why are goals scored? To some people the answer to this question is simple, it is one word—mistakes. To others it is complex because they believe there are literally hundreds of reasons why goals are scored.

There are, in fact, five basic fundamental reasons why goals are scored. Sometimes, of course, there is a combination of factors, but it is a combination of two or more of the five basic factors.

What are these factors?
(1) Lack of pressure on the man with the ball.
(2) Lack of support for the challenging player.
(3) Failure to track players down.
(4) Giving the ball away.
(5) Set plays.

(1) Lack of pressure on the man with the ball

Lack of pressure means that the defender is standing too far away from the man with the ball to prevent his passing the ball forward.

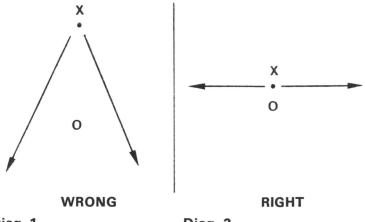

WRONG   **RIGHT**

Diag. 1   **Diag. 2**

In diagram 1 O is standing too far away from X to prevent his passing the ball forward. In diagram 2 O is standing very much nearer to X, a maximum of two yards away, and in consequence

Nottingham Forest striker Trevor Francis dives in to head past Malmo goalkeeper Jan Moeller to score the only goal of the 1979 European Cup Final in Munich.

X cannot pass the ball forward, he can only pass the ball square or backwards of square. O therefore will be able to retain his position on the goal-side of the ball.

Without question, lack of pressure on the man with the ball is the primary cause of goals and, therefore, the major deficiency in defensive play.

Pressurising will be considered in much greater detail in Chapter Three.

(2) Lack of support for the challenging player

One of the reasons why challenging players do not adopt a position close enough to their opponents is that they have a constant awareness of the space behind them and a concern for the consequences if their opponent dribbles past them. The presence of a supporting player, therefore, is of double value. In the first place he is there if required in the event of the challenging player being beaten. In the second place he can and will give the challenging player the confidence and encouragement to move in close on his opponent.

The supporting player should always be nearer to his own goal than the challenging player. His job is to challenge for the ball and win it if the challenging player is beaten.

The most common fault amongst supporting players is to position level or square with the challenging player. Often the two players are square and there is neither challenge nor support. One pass or dribble, therefore, beats both players.

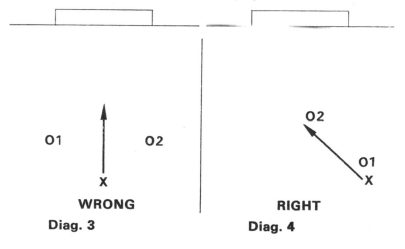

WRONG

RIGHT

Diag. 3

Diag. 4

In diagram 3 O_1 and O_2 are positioned level or square with each other. In consequence X can pass the ball or dribble the ball between them. In doing so he beats both players.

In diagram 4 O_1 is challenging X and O_2 is in a supporting position nearer to his own goal than O_1. If O_1 is beaten O_2 can move in and challenge X for the ball.

Defensive support will be considered in greater detail along with other key factors in defence in Chapter Four.

(3) Failure to track players down

Failure to track players down is failure to run with opponents and keep goal-side of them.

This quality in defending is becoming more and more important as modern strategy develops. It is common in modern football to see teams playing with three or four players in mid-field and just two or sometimes three forward players. There is, therefore, even greater importance placed upon mid-field players who can move forward into advanced positions and score goals. One of the best players in world football in this role is Martin Peters of England. He has amply demonstrated how devastating mid-field players can be when they move forward into advanced positions.

Defenders, therefore, must be watchful of any player who moves forward or who threatens the back of the defence.

A defender who tracks down his opponent must be in a position to challenge for the ball should it be played to his opponent. It is a major fault amongst defenders in general to allow opponents to get behind and goal side of them.

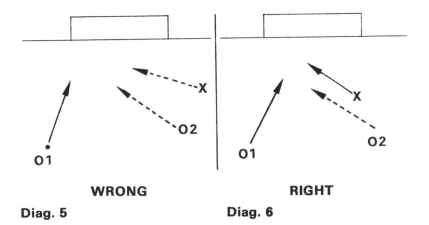

WRONG

RIGHT

Diag. 5

Diag. 6

In diagram 5 X is not on the goal-side of O_2. He is, therefore, in a very poor position to challenge for the ball and O_2 should be first to any ball played towards the goal.

In diagram 6 X is in a much better position. He is on the goal-side of O_2 and now he is in a good position to challenge O_2 for any ball which is played towards the goal.

Tracking players down will be dealt with in much more detail in Chapter Four. Suffice here to record that failure to track players who make a run towards goal is a major cause of goals and this source of goals is increasing as modern tactical developments place more emphasis on mid-field players accepting goal scoring responsibilities.

(4) Giving the ball away

At all levels of football more goals are scored through giving the ball away than most people realise. Call it mistakes, carelessness, it matters not—the effect is the same, the opposition is usually given an excellent chance of scoring, especially if the ball is given away in the defending third of the field.

The moral here is that if you must lose possession of the ball lose it in the attacking third of the field rather than the defending third of the field. A further question is posed: What is good football? Some players and some coaches think that intricate close passing in the vicinity of one's own goal is good football. This type of play often involves undue risks in which case it is inefficient football and, therefore, bad football. It should be understood that there are times when to play the ball into the grandstand is the correct thing to do. If it is correct it is good football.

Giving the ball away will be analysed in greater detail in Chapter Four. Experienced players must not assume, however, that it is only schoolboys who are prone to give the ball away. It happens at all levels from the World Cup down and indeed the opening goal of the World Cup Final in 1966 came as a result of an England player heading the ball down to Haller of West Germany who scored from twelve yards range.

(5) Set plays

This refers to goals scored from corners, free kicks and throw-ins. Forty per cent of goals are scored from set plays. It sounds an astonishing figure. But remember, these are occasions when it is not possible to exert close pressure on the man with the ball. These are also the occasions when many defenders lose their concentration and fail to do any sort of defensive job.

Many teams do not seem to appreciate the importance of set plays. One sees a general lack of organisation and planning at set plays. It is folly to spend endless hours practising passing and ball control if one then loses the match from bad marking at a corner, free kick or throw in.

It is possible to play the percentages on set plays and predict which type of play is the most likely to produce goals. This we shall go into in detail both from an attacking and a defending point of view in Chapters Nine and Ten.

CONCLUSION AND SUMMARY

Now we know why goals are scored we have an appreciation of the size of the problem. We can now consider how to pressurise support etc. We shall discover also that Association Football is a game of opposites and that, for example, having learned how to pressurise in defence we must consider how to relieve pressure in attack. Therein lies the real basis and attraction of the game. Therein also lies the major purpose of this book—to identify key factors in developing effective strategy and in developing effective team-work.

Keep constantly in mind the five fundamental reasons why goals are scored :—

(1) Lack of pressure on the man with the ball.
(2) Lack of support for the challenging player.
(3) Failure to track players down.
(4) Giving the ball away.
(5) Set plays.

CHAPTER 3

PRESSURISING

The purpose of pressurising is to decrease both the time and the space which an attacking player has in which to make his pass or his dribble.

To be effective the pressurising player should be on the goal-side of the player with the ball at a distance of not more than two yards. The pressurising player should always remember that his job wherever possible, is to keep the opposition playing in front of him and deny the opportunity for the opponent to pass the ball forward. Of course, it should be recognised immediately that it is not always possible for the pressurising player either to get goal-side or to prevent the opponent with the ball from passing the ball forward. Later in this chapter we shall consider how best to defend in these circumstances.

It must be understood, however, that it is not possible to pressurise opponents from distances of five and ten yards. Two yards from the man with the ball is the distance to aim for.

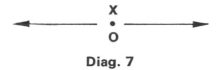

Diag. 7

O is two yards from X and X is forced to play in front of O. That is good defending.

Vital moment when the ball changes hands

As soon as the ball is lost all players in a team must think in terms of defending and should work hard immediately to win back the ball. Unfortunately, many forwards lose vital seconds when the ball is lost and they often give defenders both time and space in which to pass the ball. Defenders are not entitled to have that time and space, and forwards should ensure that they don't get it. Forwards, however, are human. Sometimes they have worked hard

Manchester United's Sammy McIlroy avoids a lunging tackle from Arsenal substitute Steve Walford and shoots the dramatic second goal for United in the 88th minute of the 1979 FA Cup Final. But Arsenal scored the winner a minute later through Alan Sunderland.

Liverpool's Alan Hansen (left) clashes with Arsenal defender Willie Young.

physically in running into a good attacking position only to see an inaccurate pass present the ball to the opposition. Sometimes they see a tremendous shot saved or they miss an easy chance and hold their head in shame. All these reactions which are normal and human amount to the same thing: the player loses his concentration. If a player has made a bad pass or he has missed an easy chance, that is an end of it. The most important thing is to concentrate upon winning the ball back. Remember this:—

Pressurising should start the moment the ball is lost. It is at this moment, when the ball changes hands, that some players lose their concentration. Football, like most games, is a game of mistakes and a primary cause of mistakes is lack of concentration.

This is a skill and teams should have plenty of practice at dealing with situations when the ball changes hands. This practice will be all the more beneficial if it takes place in an eleven-a-side game.

The recovery run

Before a player can challenge for the ball he must recover either level with the man with the ball or preferably on the goal-side of the man with the ball. It is, however, a mistake to recover too far beyond the ball into a position where the ball can still be played forward.

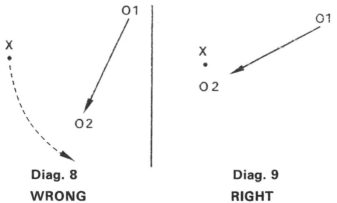

Diag. 8   **Diag. 9**
WRONG   **RIGHT**

In diagram 8 O_1 has recovered on to the goal-side of X in position O_2. But X can still pass the ball forward. O_2 therefore will quickly find that he is not in a position on the goal-side of the ball.

In diagram 9 O_1 has recovered on to the goal-side of X in position O_2 and is in a position to pressurise X and prevent him from passing the ball forward. Diagram 9 not only shows a more efficient recovery by O_2 in terms of pressurising but also an easier recovery in terms of distance run.

Recovery lines

Should a player be in doubt concerning his best line of recovery he should follow the following guide. Players on a flank should follow a line towards the near post, players in central positions should follow a line towards their penalty spot. Once a player reaches a position on the goal-side of the ball the line of recovery and marking or supporting responsibilities should be re-assessed. Defenders who are out-numbered should also retreat towards their goal. (See diagram 10)

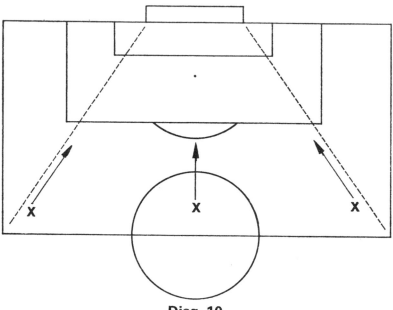

Diag. 10

Goal-side challenge for the ball

Players on the goal-side of the ball will position in such a way as to make a successful challenge for the ball possible should the ball be played to their immediate opponent. The movement to challenge of a defending player will involve two important considerations :—

(1) The speed of approach to challenge

Speed in football is not only the speed at which a player can run. It is the speed with which he makes the decision to start running. This is particularly the case in running to challenge an opponent. The time to start running is when the pass is made to one's opponent, and the time to run quickly is whilst the ball is in flight and cannot be intercepted.

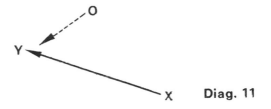

Diag. 11

In diagram 11 the pass has been made from X to Y and whilst the ball is in flight O has moved towards Y to challenge for the ball.

It is possible, however, to run too quickly or too far. The movement of O towards Y must be checked just before Y receives the ball. If O continues running quickly after Y has received the ball Y will find it easy to side step O, and O for his part will find it very difficult to change direction whilst running at speed.

(2) The angle of challenge

There are four possibilities in challenging for the ball :—

(a) **Interception.** If the defender feels that he can intercept the pass then this is the most effective way in which to win the ball and his angle of challenge will take him into the line of the pass. In diagram 12 O has moved forward to intercept

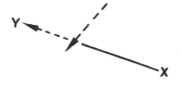

Diag. 12

the pass from X to Y. Obviously the earlier in flight he can make his interception the more likely he is to gain time and space for himself.

(b) **Tackling.** If the defender feels that he can reach his opponent as his opponent receives the ball then his angle of challenge will be in a direct line from his starting position to his opponent as illustrated in diagram 13.

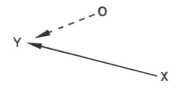

Diag. 13

(c) **Forcing the player outside.** If the defender wishes to force his opponent outside, or in the case of a full back challenging a winger, down the line, then the angle of challenge will be to cut off the route inside as illustrated in diagram 14.

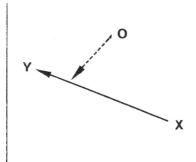

Diag. 14

(d) **Forcing the player inside.** If the defender wishes to force his opponent inside then the angle of challenge will be to cut off the route outside or down the line as illustrated in diagram 15.

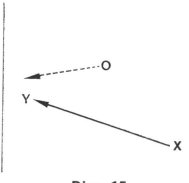

Diag. 15

Players who are pressurising opponents should adopt a position which will allow them to turn quickly. It is important that the defender should turn through 90° not 180°. The player who has to turn through 180° will be one yard slower over the first five yards. If one should doubt this then it is worth conducting a little test. Have two players run against each other over a distance of five yards. One player should start with his back to the start line, therefore making it necessary for him to turn through 180°. The second player should start with his feet parallel to the start line or at 90° to the start line, therefore making it necessary for him to turn through 90°. The player turning through 90° will win a race over five yards by one yard. Furthermore, a player who has to turn through 180° is very badly balanced and is likely to fall over in his attempt to turn quickly.

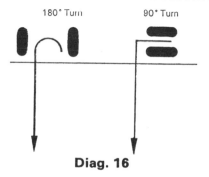

Diag. 16

Defenders must be able to turn quickly and they must also be well balanced. It is important, therefore, that they should learn early how best to challenge for the ball and how important it is to avoid being turned through 180°.

The importance of staying on your feet

When challenging for the ball it is vital for a player to stay on his feet. Players who go to ground unnecessarily, albeit for only a few seconds, reduce their team for that period to ten effective players. This is called 'selling yourself'. It should further be realised that players who go to ground frequently make the game so much harder physically. Getting up off the ground is hard work and, of course, having got up the player has to chase the opponent who should not have required chasing.

There are two occasions when it is excusable for a player to go to ground in order to win the ball:—

(i) When the opponent is clear of the defence. This is an emergency situation and any defender is entitled to adopt emergency measures and slide tackle his opponent to win the ball.

(ii) When the opponent is near to the goal-line or the touch-line and the defender in going to ground plays the ball dead and thereby is afforded time in which to recover his position.

For the greater part, however, remember that good defenders stay on their feet and that it is only fools who rush in, where good defenders fear to tread.

Prevent opponents from turning with the ball

It is important, particularly for rear defenders, to prevent opponents from turning with the ball. Defenders who allow opponents to turn with the ball present the opportunity for the opponent to pass the ball forward. Defenders who try and win the ball whilst the opponent is facing his own goal run a very great risk of giving away unnecessary free kicks. It is normally sufficient for the defender to be close enough to his opponent to challenge for the ball in the event of his attempting to turn with the ball.

Forwards who come away from defenders to receive the ball must not be allowed free space.

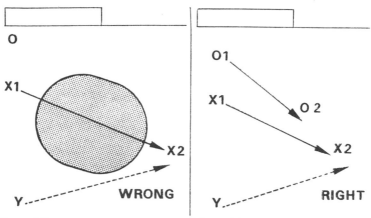

Diag. 17   **Diag. 18**

In diagram 17 X_1 has moved to position X_2 to receive a pass from Y. O has retained his position and allowed space to be created between himself and X_2. This is wrong because X_2 can now pass the ball forward.

In diagram 18 X_1 has again moved to position X_2 to receive a pass from Y but this time O has moved to position O_2. This is correct. The position at O_2 is on the goal-side of X_2 and close enough to exert pressure.

The only occasions when O would not be correct in adopting this position would be if O had a team mate free in front of him who would be better positioned to pick up the marking at X_2.

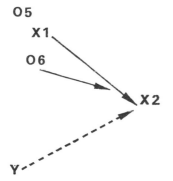

In diagram 19 X_1 has moved to position X_2. O_5, however, has retained his position since O_6 is in a good position to deal with X at position X_2.

Diag. 19

The other occasion when O will retain his position is when the opposition has created a numerical advantage against him. In these circumstances O will be more concerned with the space behind him and less concerned with the space in front. Indeed in these circumstances he will think in terms of retreat towards his goal.

If it is impossible to prevent the opponent from turning with the ball the next best thing for the defender to do is to deny the opportunity to pass the ball forward. This he can only do, however, if he is on the goal-side of the ball at a distance of not more than two yards.

Reducing the angles through which opponents can pass the ball

If play cannot be kept in front of the defence then it is best to force the play to continue in one direction. By this means it is possible to reduce the angles through which opponents can pass the ball and thereby the passing possibilities become fewer because there are fewer targets to aim at. Because the play is now predictable the marking can be tighter and the winning of the ball is made very much easier.

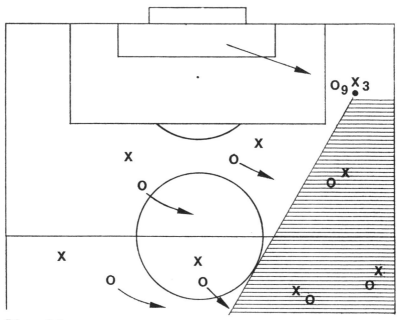

Diag. 20

In diagram 20, O_9 is challenging X_3. It is impossible for O_9 to achieve a position on the goal side of X_3 but by his position of challenge he has reduced the angle through which X_3 can pass the ball to approximately 45°. The number of targets for X_3 to pass to are also reduced to three. X_3 can only effectively pass the ball therefore inside the shaded area. It is now possible for all the O team to mark tight in the shaded area and players outside the shaded area can move round confidently into covering positions.

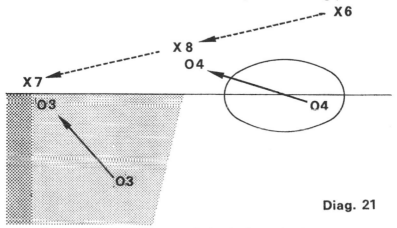

Diag. 21

In diagram 21 X_6 has passed the ball to X_8. O_4 moves in to challenge and immediately reduces the angle through which X_8 can play to less than 90° and, in addition, forces the play to continue in the same direction, i.e. to the right hand side—(the light shaded area). X_8 passes the ball to X, who is challenged by O_3 who also forces the play into a narrow area (dark shaded) down the line.

It has already been suggested that Association Football is a game of opposites. In attacking play the objective is to be inventive and unpredictable. One important way of achieving this is to change the direction of play. The task of defenders therefore is the opposite. To keep the play predictable and force the play to continue in one direction.

I hope one can begin to see from this that defence is not necessarily dull and boring. Indeed it can be fascinating, from a tactical point of view, to watch a high class display of effective defence.

Determination

There comes a time, of course, when a player must move in to win the ball. Having made the decision to win the ball a player's greatest asset is determination. It is one against one—all for the winner and nothing for the loser.

Nottingham Forest's John Robertson (right) shoots past Coventry City defender Andy Blair, but the ball went wide.

Team-work and fitness

Team-work and fitness are the basis of good pressurising. What players do as individuals is important but it is what players do as a team which is vital. There is no point in one player pressurising opponents, if the remainder of the team is not prepared to pressurise. Furthermore, if players are not prepared to run, pressurising is not possible.

Importance of compactness

If teams allow themselves to get stretched from goal to goal then vast spaces will emerge between and behind players and pressurising will not be possible.

In order to pressurise successfully, therefore, a team must avoid being stretched. A team must work hard to gain and retain compactness. This they will do in three ways :—

FIRST—by forward players working hard to recover and exert pressure the moment the ball is lost.

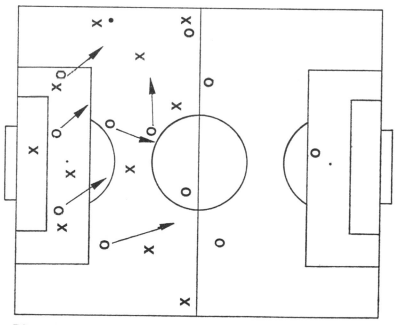

Diag. 22

In diagram 22 it can be seen that the forward players in the O team are working hard to recover and mark players and put the whole of the X team under pressure.

SECOND—by rear and mid-field players moving up when the ball is played forward.

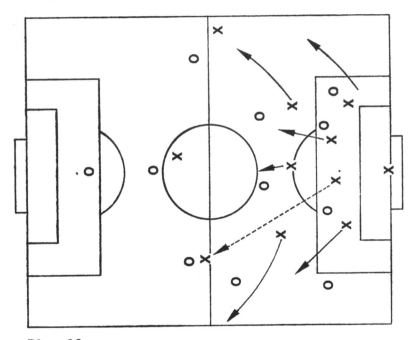

Diag. 23

When the ball is played forward, particularly to one of the front players, it is vital to move forward quickly to give support to the player with the ball. If the ball is then lost at least there is a space and time restriction on one's opponents. It is quite common, of course, for forward players who have lost the ball to recover slowly when the defence moves up to support their own forward players. Often two players will be in off-side positions. It should be appreciated, therefore, that by moving forward quickly the effective opposition can be reduced to nine or even eight players. This must not be confused with off-side tactics. It is not done with the purpose of catching players off-side, although as we now see that may be one of the results. Nor is there a risk involved so long as your team is in possession of the ball. It is, in fact, a good example of positive team thinking.

THIRD—by players moving across field when the opposition has possession of the ball on a flank in order to lock the ball in that quarter of the field.

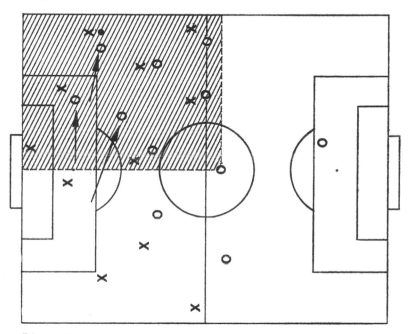

Diag. 24

In diagram 24 it can be seen how the O team have moved across and, excluding the goalkeepers, the numerical situation in the right hand quarter is Six X v Seven O. In the left hand quarter the numerical situation is four X v three O. Provided the O team, therefore, can keep the ball locked on their right flank they have a numerical advantage where they require it. It should further be appreciated that although the X team has a numerical advantage on the left hand side of the field this is because two of the X back players have been left free. These are the players least likely to move forward into advanced positions.

CONCLUSION AND SUMMARY

Lack of pressure is the most important single cause of goals being scored. It therefore follows that good pressurising both as individuals and as a team is the most important single defensive factor.

Try and remember the following key points:—

(1) Concentrate on your job when the ball changes hands.
(2) Consider your recovery run. *Don't* recover too far beyond the ball.
(3) Remember the best line of recovery if you are in doubt.
(4) When challenging for the ball on the goal-side remember:—
    (i) The speed of approach.
    (ii) The angle of challenge.
(5) Stay on your feet.
(6) Try and prevent opponents from turning with the ball.
(7) If you cannot prevent them from turning deny them the opportunity to pass the ball forward.
(8) If you cannot prevent them from passing the ball forward try and reduce the angles through which they can play.
(9) Be determined in challenging for the ball.
(10) Remember the importance of fitness and team-work.
(11) Remember the importance of compactness and the three ways in which a team will achieve compactness.

CHAPTER 4

KEY FACTORS IN DEFENSIVE PLAY

There are four key factors in defending. The most important of these factors, pressurising opponents, has been considered in Chapter Three. The other three factors are :—
(1) Defensive support.
(2) Tracking players down.
(3) Attacking the ball under pressure.

(1) Defensive support

Defensive support is required for the player pressurising the man with the ball. If the pressurising player is beaten then it is the responsibility of the supporting player to exert pressure immediately.

The first consideration, therefore, for a supporting player is his distance from the pressurising or challenging player since he must decrease both the time and the space in which an attacking player has to work once he has beaten the initial challenge.

Distance from the pressurising player

The ideal distance is four to six yards away from the challenging player. From this distance it will be possible to achieve two objectives.
(a) Limit time and space for the opponent to work in.
(b) The supporting player will be close enough to challenge immediately if the challenging player is beaten.

However, there are other considerations. If the opponent is very fast it is possible that he could play the ball past both the pressurising and the supporting players and win a race to the ball. Much depends on the defensive arrangement of other players and also the area of the field. In the middle third of the field, and especially on a flank, there is a greater possibility of a winger for example, trying to beat both the challenging and the supporting player for speed.

A supporting player, therefore, must consider three factors before deciding how near or far he should be from the challenging player :—
(a) The positions of other defending players.
(b) The abilities of the opponent in possession of the ball, i.e. does he like to kick the ball ahead and sprint past opponents ? If so, support from a little further away. Does he like to bring the ball up to opponents and dribble past them ? If so, move up in close support of the challenging player.
(c) The area of the field.

Having made those points it is worth stressing that the major fault amongst supporting players is that they support from too far away.

The angle of the supporting player

The second consideration in selecting a defensive support position is the angle of the supporting player from the pressurising player. There are three possible positions.

(A) When the opponent is being forced down the line. The position is just backward of straight as shown in diagram 25.

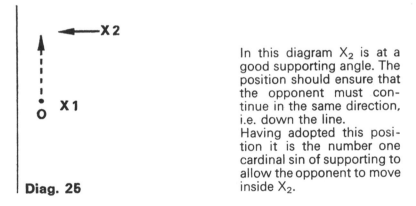

In this diagram X_2 is at a good supporting angle. The position should ensure that the opponent must continue in the same direction, i.e. down the line.
Having adopted this position it is the number one cardinal sin of supporting to allow the opponent to move inside X_2.

Diag. 25

(B) When the opponent is being forced across the field the position is just backward of square as illustrated in diagram 26.

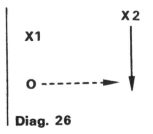

Again the opponent must be made to continue in one direction — in this case across the field, and must be denied the opportunity of passing or dribbling the ball towards goal.

Diag. 26

Argentina's Hugo Villeverde (2) dives in to head clear. The midfield man Osvaldo Ardiles has taken up a position on the edge of the penalty area to collect the ball as it comes out.

Birmingham City's Gordon Taylor has beaten Coventry City's John Craven, but Graham Oakey has moved round to cover, and cut out the cross.

(C) If in doubt select a position at 45° as illustrated in diagram 27.

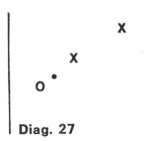

Diag. 27

This is particularly the case if the pressurising player is not tight enough. In these circumstances the opponent could go either way and the duty of the supporting player is to try and position to give himself a chance of dealing with either possibility.

Responsibilities of the supporting player

The responsibility of the supporting player is to position himself at the correct distance and the correct angle and also to pass on all necessary information to the pressurising player. The supporting player must encourage the pressurising player to move in close on his opponent. The supporting player should also indicate whether the opponent should be forced outside or inside.

It is important that teams should practice supporting as a team. They must, most of all, agree the language. When a player gives the instruction 'force him outside', it should be clearly understood where outside is. It is an amazing thing, but what is outside to one player is often inside to another. This is yet another example of the importance of team-work. Players should also be encouraged and given practice at moving in close support. Young players particularly should be given clearly to understand that the biggest fault in supporting is supporting from too far away from the pressurising player.

(2) Tracking players down

Defending players who allow attackers to move into positions behind them make a great mistake. Defending players who do not see opponents move into positions behind them make an even greater mistake.

Keep goal-side of your opponent

This is the first rule in tracking players down. It is not always understood what is meant by goal-side.

In diagram 28 O is not on the goal-side of X_2 he is, in fact, on the corner flag side and will lose a race against X_2 for the ball played in front of goal.

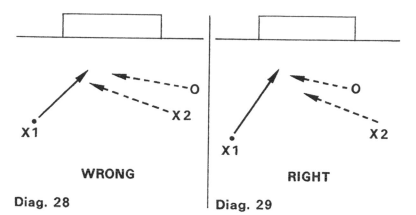

WRONG

Diag. 28

RIGHT

Diag. 29

In diagram 29 O is correctly positioned on the goal-side of X_2 and will win a race against X_2 for the ball played in front of goal.

Keep the ball and opponents in view

The second rule in tracking players down is to keep both the ball and the opposing player in view. Defenders who watch the ball to the exclusion of players are referred to as 'ball watchers'. These players invite opponents to get behind them.

There is at least one similarity in the techniques of being a good defender and being a good driver of a motor car. In each case it is not only important to know what is going on in front of you, but equally important to know what is happening behind.

Good defenders are constantly glancing over their shoulders and adjusting their positions in relation to the movement of opposing players.

Players require frequent practice at tracking players down and a very useful practice is to have a small-sided game of man-to-man marking. This makes players look for their opponents and keep them under constant survey.

The point has been made in Chapter Two that modern tactics are placing more and more emphasis on mid-field and rear players moving forward and accepting responsibility for scoring goals. It is, therefore, important that both forward and mid-field players should realise their defensive responsibilities. If players would watch for opponents making a forward run and then track them down immediately, in many cases they would deter their opponent within a few yards. Players moving forward are given great encouragement if they are left to run free of challenge. Players who are tracked in their run, and this applies particularly to rear players, quickly become nervous of the space left behind them.

If forward and mid-field players in particular would realise this and work hard to deter their opponents from making this type of run, in the long term they would save themselves a great deal of running.

(3) Attacking the ball under pressure

It is a fact that at every level of football goals are scored because defenders fail to clear the ball. In the vicinity of their own goal it is vital that defenders should attack the ball in a manner which will gain time for the defence. Defenders under the pressure of a forceful attack will have four objectives in clearing the ball :—

(a) Be first to the ball.
(b) Go for height.
(c) Go for distance.
(d) Play the ball wide.

(a) **Be first to the ball.** It does not matter how good a player is at heading the ball or how safe his kicking, if he is not first to the ball his techniques count for nothing.

To be first to the ball one has got to move to meet the ball and one has got to take the ball as early in flight as possible, i.e. at the highest point in trajectory that one can reach.

Defenders, of course, particularly in their own penalty area, have an enormous advantage over the attackers because the ball is almost invariably coming towards them and it is, therefore, very much easier to move into the line of flight and attack the ball.

However, being first to the ball is not only a matter of technique. It is very largely a matter of determination and in the case of heading a matter of courage as well.

If players are good at attacking the ball then there is no reason why they should not also be good at clearing the ball, because the considerable force of their body momentum will always be applied to the ball.

(b) **Go for height.** Height means time and in the penalty area time favours the defence. It is better to play the ball straight up in the air, even if the ball is in the six yard area, rather than play the ball down to an opponent on the edge of the penalty area.

In order to play for height, whether it is from foot or head, the ball must be struck through the bottom half. There is no magic in this : if one strikes the ball through the bottom half the ball will go up ; if one strikes the ball through the top half the ball will go down. It is as simple as that.

Arsenal's Frank Stapleton moves in to challenge Everton's Asa Hartford.

Aston Villa defender John Gregory kicks clear.

(c) **Go for distance.** This means go for distance but only with height. Going for distance without height is of little value because in a crowded penalty area the ball will not be allowed to travel very far. The greater the distance, however, that the ball can be played away from the goal, the more likely it is that the danger to goal will be cleared.

(d) **Play the ball wide.** This is always sound advice for defenders because this should ensure that the ball is not only played a safe distance from goal but also at a reasonably safe angle.

If possible balls which are crossed from the opponent's right wing should be cleared towards the opponent's left wing and vice versa. This is because it is reasonable to expect that that area will be less heavily populated with opponents. Defenders, however, should still play the ball for height, distance and width, in that order.

It will be appreciated that there are times when it will be perfectly acceptable, indeed correct, to play the ball well over the touch line. If a player feels that he is under pressure or a team is under pressure in and around their penalty area then the ball must be cleared long and wide. Of course, some will consider this to be bad football. But this is yet another occasion for playing the percentages. Upon consideration of the percentages one will quickly realise what is good and what is correct . . . most times. Settle for that.

CONCLUSION AND SUMMARY

Defensive support, tracking players down and attacking the ball under pressure are key factors in defence and together with pressurising they constitute the big dividend factors in defensive play.

Try and remember the following points :—

(1) Defensive support.
    (a) The distance of the supporting player.
    (b) The angle of the supporting player (three possible positions).
    (c) The responsibility of the supporting player for giving information.
(2) Tracking players down.
    (a) Keep goal-side of your opponent.
    (b) Keep the ball and your opponent in view.
(3) Attacking the ball under pressure.
    (a) Be first to the ball.
    (b) Go for height.
    (c) Go for distance.
    (d) Play the ball wide.

CHAPTER 5

CREATING SPACE

A defence in retreat will funnel back towards its own goal with the primary objective of sealing off space near the goal to the attacking players.

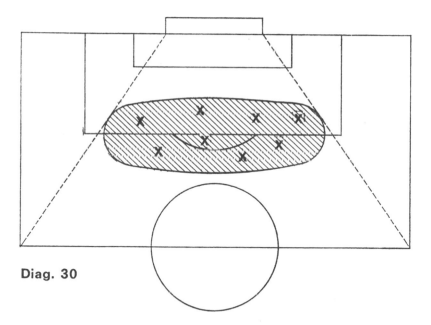

Diag. 30

Stretching the opposition from side to side

Football is a game of opposites and, therefore, having funnelled back to restrict space and win the ball the first requirement in attack is to spread out and create space by stretching the opposition from side to side.

This is another of those vital moments for concentration when the ball changes hands. Defenders having won the ball, especially rear defenders, often relax and move out from goal very casually and slowly. By doing so they win the ball but lose the initiative.

Defenders having won the ball should spread out quickly. Full-backs, for example, should think in terms of moving into wide positions and they should make their run as early and as quickly as possible.

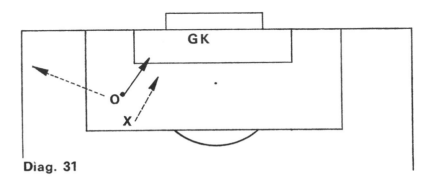

Diag. 31

In diagram 31 O has passed the ball back to his goalkeeper. If he has passed the ball correctly there is no need for him to continue along the line of pass since nothing can prevent the ball from reaching the goalkeeper. He should now make the decision to sprint into a wide position near to the touch line.

O should be on his way to this position before the G.K. has fielded the ball. Just as in the chapter on pressurising the point was made that it is important for defenders to close up on their opponents and restrict space whilst the ball is in flight, so it is equally important for attackers to move wide and create space also whilst the ball is in flight.

Defenders will get good rewards for this type of quick thinking and hard work since most attackers, like X in diagram 31, will follow the line of the ball rather than the player who is running wide.

Teams winning the ball in their own penalty area are sometimes in too great a hurry to get themselves and the ball to the other end of the field. The result is that they move out from goal but they do not spread out and create space effectively.

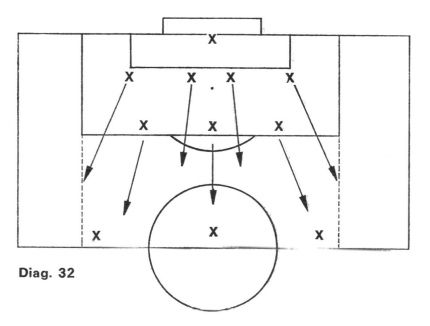

Diag. 32

In diagram 32 the seven X players have moved out from their penalty area but the whole team including the front players is playing on a maximum width of 44 yards, i.e. only the width of the penalty area. Teams who play in this manner make the task for their opponents easy. Their main job in defence is to restrict space and this has already been done for them by the very arrangement of the attacking players.

If after having won the ball attacking players spread out, opponents will find it difficult both to mark players and support each other. By stretching players from side to side space is created between players.

In diagram 33 the X team has spread out much more effectively The goalkeeper has the ball, but notice particularly the type of runs being made by X_2 and X_3. Their runs are not only wide but almost parallel with the goal-line. This will almost certainly help to create more space for X_7 and X_{11} who are also moving into wide positions.

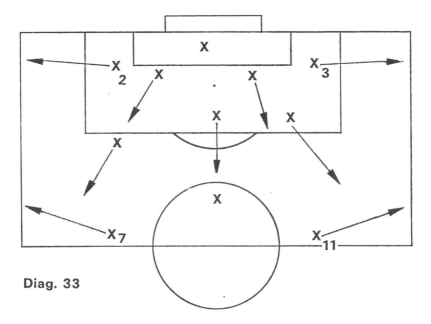

Diag. 33

When players are asked to move into a wide position they invariably interpret this as fifteen yards inside the touch line. Wide means going to the touch line. It is also a fault for the player with the ball, and in these situations it is frequently the goalkeeper, to pass the ball before the player has reached his position. The result is twofold: either the player stops to receive the ball in a position which is less than wide, or the ball is intercepted because the ball is short of pace and fails to reach the player who continues his run into a wide position. It will prove helpful to remember the following points in relation to stretching opponents from side-to-side:—

    (1) Make the decision to move wide early and try and cover as much ground as possible whilst the ball is in flight.

    (2) Move fast.

    (3) Wide means very wide—on the touch-line.

    (4) Full-backs will almost invariably take the short route wide, which means running parallel with the goal-line.

    (5) Try and delay the service of the ball until you know the player has achieved his wide position.

Stretching opponents end to end

It is also important to stretch players from end to end in order to create space either in front of or behind opponents.

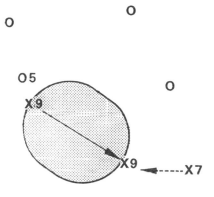

Diag. 34

In diagram 34 X_9 has moved to meet the pass from X_7, but O_5 has not followed. Space is, therefore, created (the shaded area) in front of O_5 and X_9 is in a position to pass the ball forward or dribble forward with the ball.

In diagram 35 O_5 has followed X_9 and this time the space created (the shaded area) is behind O_5.

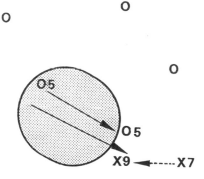

Diag. 35

In these two examples, therefore, we see that it is probable that if O_5 lets X_9 move to meet the pass unchallenged there may be a defensive problem of lack of pressure on X_9. On the other hand if O_5 follows X_9 to meet the pass there may be a problem of defensive support for O_5 because the space between the defending players is increased.

An individual running away from the player with the ball and then checking to run towards the player with the ball, or vice versa, will normally create space for himself. This is a simple technique and could be used more often to good effect.

Running past opponents will also have a similar effect of creating space between opponents.

Change of direction

Defenders will react to two things :—

(1) The movement of the ball.
(2) The movement of opponents, and possibly the movement of co-defenders in certain positions.

The more often and the quicker the point of attack is changed, the more likely it is that defenders will be caught out of position and thereby space created for attacking players.

It has already been stressed in the chapters concerning defence that a primary object of defence is to force play to continue in one direction and, therefore, make the play predictable.

The primary object of attack is the opposite: to change the direction of play, to make the play unpredictable, and to create space. How is this achieved?

(1) By moving with the ball in one direction and passing the ball in the other direction

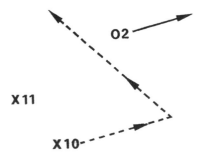

Diag. 36

In diagram 36 X_{10} dribbles the ball to the right and then passes the ball to the left. Space is created for X_{11} because O_2 will react to the movement fo X_{10} and move in-field away from X_{11}.

(2) By cross-over plays. This requires a certain expertise in timing between two players. However, the movement is basically simple : one player moves from left to right, the other player moves across him from right to left.

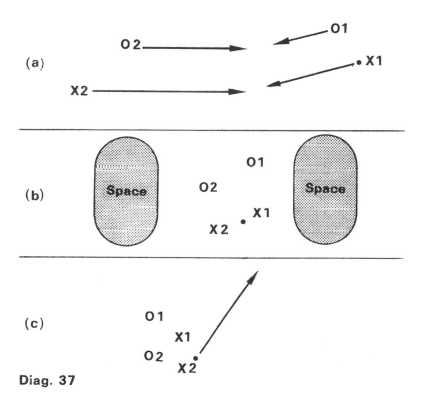

Diag. 37

In diagram 37 (a) X_1 is in possession of the ball and is moving towards X_2 from right to left. X_2 is moving towards X_1 from left to right. The players are marked by O_1 and O_2 respectively. Diagram 37 (b) shows the position just before X_2 takes the ball from X_1. Space has been created on both sides of the group of players.

Diagram 37 (c) shows X_2 taking the ball from X_1, moving into space, and passing the ball forward.

It does not matter, of course, which player moves away with the ball. It would be just as easy for X_1 to move away with the ball, but at the moment the players actually cross there should be an acceleration of pace not only in order for the player with the ball to get free but also for the player without the ball to attract either or both players towards him. It should be emphasised that the player dribbling the ball, in this case X_1, should screen the ball from his opponent. In the example of diagram 37 X_1 would dribble the ball on his left foot rather than his right foot.

There are, of course, a number of variations on the theme of cross-over plays and they are all particularly effective against a defence which is trying to force the play in one direction. Time spent in practising cross-over plays will never be wasted.

(3) Playing the ball quickly. All teams should practise playing one touch football. This is not only because one touch is the quickest way of passing the ball but because it is important that players should learn to play with their heads up observing what is happening around them. Nothing will achieve that quicker or more effectively than one touch football.

But one touch football is a means of changing the point of attack and moving the ball far quicker than defenders can adjust their positions. It is, therefore, the best means of creating space, literally out of nothing. It is not without significance that the team which plays one touch football more effectively than any other in world class football is Brazil. This has not happened by accident nor by some divine gift bestowed on the Brazilians. It has happened by design and practice. Go thou and do likewise.

To play at a high level teams must be capable of playing accurate one touch football. The nearer one gets to one's opponent's goal the more important it is to have the capacity for playing the ball quickly and accurately.

(4) Disguise. One hallmark of an outstanding player in Association Football is the ability to disguise his intentions. Effective disguise makes an opponent move in anticipation of a pass or a dribble and thus space is created for the attacking player.

All players should try and make their play, particularly their passing, less predictable. In this respect passes which are made with the side of the foot are more predictable than passes which are made with the instep. Of course, one realises that most players pass the ball with the side of the foot because they feel they will be more accurate. These players should understand, however, that because these passes are easier for defenders to 'read' or predict, they also make defenders more accurate in their positional play.

It is worth practising passing with the instep in order to make one's play just that little bit less predictable.

(5) Dribbling. The player who can beat an opponent by dribbling past him creates space by putting an opponent out of the game. Players who have the skill to do this are invaluable in a team since they can create space and trouble for the opposition when neither space nor trouble existed. It is important, however, for these players to remember when to use their skill of dribbling. They will prove an enormous asset if they use their skill successfully in the attacking third of the field, but in the defending third of the field anything less than 100% success is likely to reduce them to a liability.

(6) Good ball control. The player whose ball control is not so good needs more space in which to make his control than the player whose control is very good. There are two factors involved in achieving good ball control. The first is to understand the principles of control: the second is to practise. No book can help with the second factor and one should be always mindful that the ingredients for success are one ounce of information to one ton of practice. Here then is the ounce of information on the principles of good ball control:—

  (a) Move into the line of flight. If a player fails to do this he will fail to make a contact with the ball.
  (b) Select early the controlling surface. Decide whether you are going to control the ball with chest or thigh or foot etc. Decide early, and having decided do not change your mind.
  (c) Withdraw the controlling surface on impact. This is rather like a boxer riding a punch.
  (d) Relax the controlling surface. If the surface is not relaxed it will be rigid and the ball will bounce away. When players are afraid of missing their control they fail to relax, become tense and they then do themselves less than justice. So relax and enjoy yourself!

CONCLUSION AND SUMMARY

Effective attacking play is not possible without the creation of space. The greater the range of techniques which a team employs to create space the more difficult it will be for opponents to establish a composed and effective defence.

Here are some important points to remember:—

(1) Try and stretch your opponents from side-to-side.
(2) Try and stretch your opponents from end-to-end.
(3) Change of direction:—
    (a) Moving one way and passing the other way.
    (b) Cross-over plays.
(4) The importance of playing the ball quickly.
(5) The importance of disguise.
(6) Dribbling—when is it an asset? and when may it be a liability?
(7) The importance of good ball control—four principles.

CHAPTER 6

SUPPORT IN ATTACK

The purpose of support in attack from behind the ball is first to relieve the pressure on the man with the ball, and second, to do what the man with the ball cannot do, which is pass the ball forward.

Forward players in particular are likely to find themselves under pressure and the principal way in which to relieve that pressure is to support the man with the ball. Support is always important, but it is absolutely vital against a team which is pressurising well. Supporting players should understand that it is essential to the performance of their job that they move into position quickly. When a team always has the opportunity to play the ball early it is a sign that the supporting is good. It is also a fact that a team which supports well and plays the ball early is very difficult to pressurise. Conversely, of course, a team which does not support well will find it very difficult to build successful attacks. Players must appreciate quickly, therefore, when a team-mate needs support and move into position quickly.

In order to achieve a good supporting position two factors are of particular importance :—

(1) The distance of the supporting player from the man with the ball

In normal circumstances an ideal distance would be between ten and fifteen yards. This will certainly vary, however, in accordance with the area of the field. In the defending third of the field a rear player, possibly a central defender supporting a full-back, may want to be absolutely safe and support at a distance of 25 yards. This distance will give the player more time because in this equation space equals time.

On the other hand a player in the attacking third of the field may move in very close support, perhaps as near as five or six yards because it is often necessary for forwards to do their work in confined spaces and with the maximum speed.

Ground surfaces also affect supporting distances. If the ground is uneven and bumpy a supporting player will be wise to give himself a little more space because he may need more time than usual to control the ball. If the surface is good and even and the ground is firm then the supporting player may move in closer in order to do his work a little quicker.

Football pitches, like cricket wickets, are sometimes fast and sometimes slow. and the technique of playing must be adjusted to meet the requirements of the pace of the pitch. One thing is certain: it is not possible to play really quickly on a slow pitch. In this respect one questions the merit of training on hard surfaces in preparation for matches which are likely to be played in mud.

However, having due regard for the fact that the pace of pitches will vary, and even the pace of the same pitch will often vary from the centre to the flanks, the main factor in determining the pace of a game is the quality of a team's support. If a team supports well then they will control a large amount of ball possession. If a team can control ball possession then they should be able to control the pace of the game.

(2) The angle of the supporting player from the man with the ball

The second factor in the selection of a good supporting position is the angle of the supporting player from the man with the ball. There are two considerations for the supporting player in selecting the angle of his position.

The first consideration is to be at an angle where he can receive the ball.

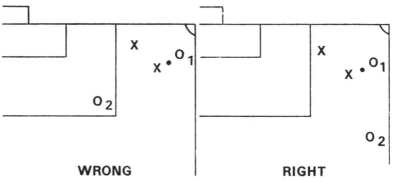

WRONG   **RIGHT**

Diag. 38   **Diag. 39**

Obviously, if the supporting player is not in a position where he can receive the ball he is not in fact supporting the player with the ball.

In diagram 38 O_2 is supporting O_1. O_2 is not, however, in a position to receive the ball and the angle of his support is, therefore, incorrect.

In diagram 39 O_2 has moved into a position at an angle where he can receive the ball and the position is therefore correct.

The second consideration is to be at an angle where the point of attack can be changed and from which the supporting player has the opportunity to pass the ball forward through as wide a range as possible.

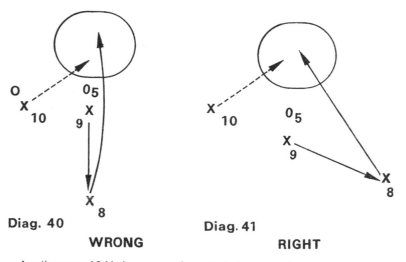

Diag. 40
WRONG

Diag. 41
RIGHT

In diagram 40 X_8 is supporting straight, therefore he is attacking along the same line as X_9. The movement of the ball from X_9 to X_8 is not likely to cause defenders trouble in their positioning. Furthermore in order to exploit the space directly behind O_5, X_8 has to play the ball over the head of O_5 thus giving himself a difficult technique. X_{10} is running into the space behind O_5 to receive the pass from X_8 and has to control a bouncing ball.

Diagram 41 shows how the whole play could be so much better. X_8 this time supports X_9 at 45° and as the ball is played to him so the point of attack is changed which will cause defenders to adjust their positions. X_8 is now at an angle from which he can pass the ball forward into the space behind O_5 and he can play the pass along the ground—a much easier technique than lofting or chipping the ball. X_{10} moving into the space behind O_5 also has a much easier ball to control and is, therefore, likely to be more efficient. This is a good example of correct angled supporting. It is also a good illustration of the fact that effective team-work is largely a question of doing the simple things well.

The angle of support is important, therefore, in order to receive the ball, in order to change the point of attack and in order to provide the best opportunity for passing the ball forward. There is no one angle which is always correct. If players are in doubt, however, they should elect to support at an angle of 45°.

The timing of Kevin Keegan's run and leap enable him to out-jump Scotland's giant defender Gordon McQueen.

When not to support

Part of the skill of being a good supporting player is to know when to support from behind the ball and when to move into a position in advance of the ball. The first question, therefore, is when should a player move into a position in advance of the ball? The answer really is that a player should move forward in advance of the ball when the player in possession of the ball no longer needs support. Of course, it would not make tactical sense for every player to try and take up positions in advance of the ball, since the defence should always be organised and ready to meet emergencies. So the defence should be organised on the basis of equal numbers, i.e. if the opposition leaves three players up we leave three players back. Some teams prefer to leave an extra player back. However, it should be appreciated that if a team is in possession of the ball it is being over cautious to hold back an extra player and, more important, it makes the task of the attacking players more difficult. Given these considerations, therefore, the time for an attacking player to move forward in advance of the ball is when the player with the ball no longer needs support.

All players, of course, when they move forward will calculate on the degree of safety or risk involved. The nearer one gets to the attacking third of the field the less the risk involved.

It is important that players should realise that if they are going forward, this means in advance of the ball not level with the ball.

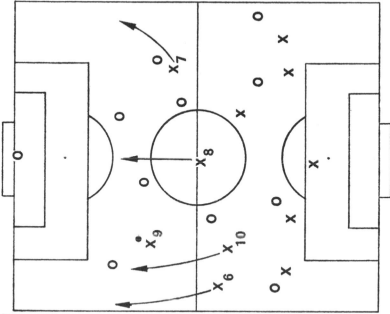

Diag. 42

In diagram 42 the X team is attacking and X_9 has possession of the ball. He is in the middle third of the field and he has no X player in advance of him. He has plenty of support from X_6, X_{10} and X_8 but he does not need support. All three of these players, X_6, X_{10} and X_8 must work hard to get into positions in advance of X_9.

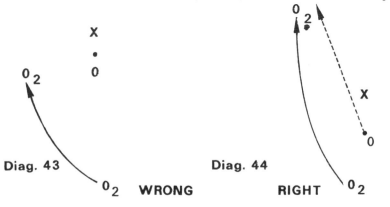

Diag. 43 **WRONG**

Diag. 44 **RIGHT**

In diagram 43 O_2 has only moved level with the ball and, therefore, O cannot pass the ball forward. This is wrong. In diagram 44 O_2 has done much better and run into a position in advance of the ball and has made it possible for O to pass the ball forward past X. This is correct.

Players moving forward should constantly look for spaces behind opponents and in the final third of the field players should look for positions from which a strike at goal is possible.

CONCLUSION AND SUMMARY

Good supporting from behind the ball is the basis of good attacking play and will ensure that a team has plenty of ball possession. But that is not enough. Ball possession must be used as a means for producing strikes on the opponent's goal. In this respect players who know when to support and when to move forward in advance of the ball are invaluable.

Try and remember the following points :—

(1) The distance of the supporting player from the man with the ball.
(2) The angle of the supporting player from the man with the ball.
(3) When not to support.
(4) The importance of moving in advance of the ball and into the space behind opponents.

CHAPTER 7

ATTACKING OPPONENTS WITH AND WITHOUT THE BALL

When a team gains possession of the ball the whole team must think positively in terms of attacking the opposition and, of course, the player with the ball must think positively of attacking the opposition also.

There are three ways in which the player in possession of the ball can attack the opposition :—

(1) By passing the ball

The player in possession of the ball will attack the opposition by passing the ball forward, especially if the ball goes past one or more than one opponent. It should be clearly understood that if a player has the opportunity to pass the ball forward and fails to do so then he has played unskilfully. Some players, of course, are constantly looking to pass the responsibility rather than the ball.

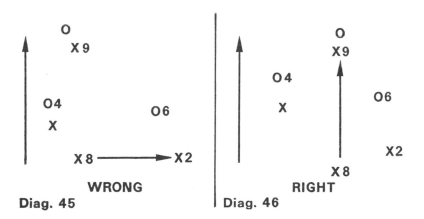

WRONG

Diag. 45

RIGHT

Diag. 46

In diagram 45 X_8 has passed the ball to X_2 who is in no better position than X_8. X_8 could have passed the ball forward and has played in an unskilful manner.

In diagram 46 X_8 has passed the ball to X_9 and in so doing has beaten O_4 and O_6 X_8 has made the correct pass and has played in a skilful manner.

Good and bad passing is related to the area of the field in which the pass is made. What may be a good pass in one area of the field may be a bad pass in another area of the field. In the end, passes are calculated on the degree of safety or risk involved. In the attacking third of the field a player should be prepared to take risks by, if necessary, trying difficult techniques and passing the ball through narrow angles and into small spaces. In the attacking third of the field the dividends are high and, therefore, the passer of the ball will calculate on the side of risk. On the other hand, in the defending third of the field, a player should calculate on the side of safety for the obvious reason that to take risks in that part of the field would be to court disaster. In many ways, therefore, it is in the middle third of the field that a player must calculate and balance the risk and safety factors of passing most carefully.

It should further be realised that passing is an obvious factor for playing the percentages. In the defending third of the field it is not unreasonable to expect players to be 100% accurate in their passing. In the final third of the field, however, a player who can achieve 25% success when playing the ball behind the defence is doing extremely well. Players should also realise that it is in the attacking third of the field that one really needs a wide range of techniques and the confidence to use them.

Passing is the most important skill of all, because it is the one used most often during a game. Time spent practising passing will never be wasted. Here are four principles which will help to produce more accurate passing :—

(a) Accuracy

Most players are accurate when passing the ball twenty-five yards or less without opposition. The problem is being accurate when one has to assess the positions of opponents and one's own players. A player must be able to pass the ball accurately. If he cannot do so without opposition he is unlikely to do so when there are opponents. In these circumstances a player must work hard, if necessary on his own, in order to become accurate. If, however, a player is accurate without opposition there is no purpose served by continuing to practise without opposition. He must now be involved in the judgment of assessing the positions and movements of co-operating and opposing players.

(b) Timing of release

Some players release their passes too soon and the player for whom the pass was intended never reaches the ball. Other players release their passes too late and invariably the ball never reaches its target because it is blocked. A few, a rare group, always seem to release their passes at exactly the right moment. Timing the release of the pass involves good judgment of the positions of co-operating and opposing players. It is not possible to develop this judgment without frequent practice against opposing players and with co-operating players. Small-sided games, 2 v 1 and 3 v 2 situations, are also helpful in providing the practice situation to develop this judgment.

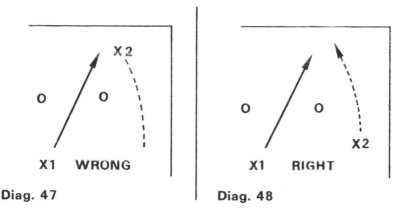

Diag. 47   X1 WRONG

Diag. 48   X1 RIGHT

In diagram 47 X_1 has allowed X_2 to run into an off-side position before releasing the ball. The timing of the release of the pass is, therefore, too late.

In diagram 48 X_1 has passed the ball whilst X_2 was still on-side The timing of the release is, therefore, correct.

(c) Pacing of the pass

This is a technique which is particularly important when a player is playing to space rather than to a player's feet. Some players pass the ball too hard, with too much pace, and the ball is sent far beyond the target. Other players pass the ball too softly, with insufficient pace, and the ball is invariably intercepted. Some players, again only a few, have the ability to pass the ball at the correct pace.

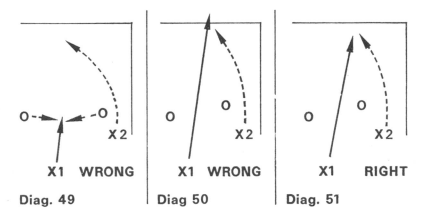

X1 WRONG   X1 WRONG   X1   RIGHT

Diag. 49   **Diag 50**   **Diag. 51**

In diagram 49 X_1 has passed the ball with insufficient pace to beat the two O players. In consequence the ball is intercepted. This is poor pacing of the pass.

In diagram 50 X_1 has passed the ball with too much pace and the ball has gone over the goal-line before X_2 could reach the ball. This also is poor pacing of the pass.

In diagram 51 X_1 has put enough pace on the ball to beat both O players but not too much to send the ball over the goal-line. In consequence X_2 reaches the ball in a good position behind both O players. This is good judgment of pace.

(d) Disguise

This is one clear hallmark of a very good player—the ability to make opponents think you are going to do one thing and then doing another. By this means opponents who are in the line of a pass are caused to move out of the line in anticipation, and then the ball is played through the vacant gap. Disguise requires confidence but this will only come about through practice against opponents.

In games where the marking is tight the ability to disguise will enable a player to create space and passing opportunities where neither space nor passing opportunities existed. Players who can disguise their intentions are very difficult to play against.

It will be appreciated now that passing must be practised against opponents and with co-operating players. Most players are accurate in cold blood and inaccurate in matches. The manner in which a player practises is all important.

(2) By dribbling the ball

Passing is usually better than dribbling because it is quicker. This is especially true in the middle third of the field. However, players who can attack opponents by dribbling past them are invaluable in a team. Two vital points should be remembered :—

(a) Run straight at your opponent with the ball.

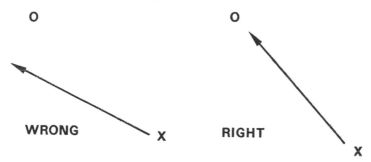

Diag. 52   **Diag. 53**

In diagram 52 X has run to the side of O. This in no way places O in an embarrassing position and is wrong.

In diagram 53 X has run straight at O. O is now totally committed to defend against X and will be embarrassed by the positive play of X which is correct.

(b) Play the ball past your opponent.

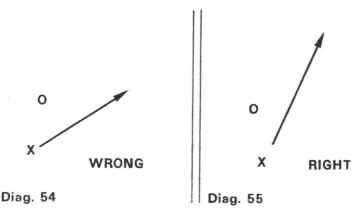

Diag. 54   Diag. 55

Spurs' Osvaldo Ardiles glides past a lunging tackle from Birmingham City's Archie Gemmill.

In diagram 54 X, when just outside tackling range, plays the ball to the side of O. O is, therefore, able to adjust his position and keep goal-side of the ball. This is poor play by X.

In diagram 55 X, when just outside tackling range, plays the ball past O and will beat O to the ball since O has to turn. This is good play by X.

Players should also try and develop the technique of slight change of direction followed by explosive change of pace as the ball is played past one's opponent. This technique involves running straight at your opponent with the ball, and when the ball is just outside tackling range the ball should be played again slightly left of straight. The defending player usually reacts to this by transferring his body weight on to his right foot. The ball is then played past his left foot and the player in an explosive change of pace sprints past his opponent.

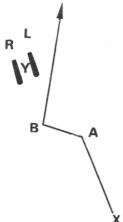

In diagram 56 X attacks Y whose feet are shown (R—right foot, L—left foot). When X reaches point A he changes direction to left of centre and Y will react by transferring his body weight on to his right foot. X from point B plays the ball past the left foot of Y and accelerates past Y.

Diag. 56

Best results are achieved by this technique if the ball is dribbled on the right foot only (rather than alternate feet) or, of course, the left foot if the player wishes to go the other way.

There is little doubt that dribbling as a technique, and as a method of attacking opponents with the ball, should be emphasised more than it is. Effective team tactics of the future will require that more players possess the ability to dribble past opponents.

One fact which will not change, however, is that dribbling will still be employed to the greatest advantage in the attacking third of the field.

(3) By shooting the ball

One is thinking here particularly of long range shots from twenty yards or more. The advantage of shots from this distance, past numerous defenders and attackers, is that the goal-keeper may be unsighted or there may be a deflection. Players should never neglect an opportunity to shoot.

It is significant that a high percentage of goals by the Brazilians are scored from outside the penalty area. Modern strategy requires that players should accept responsibility for shooting from outside the penalty area. Once again it is necessary to consider the percentages. From a situation some twenty or twenty-five yards out from goal there are three possibilities for the attacking players :—

(a) Inter-pass to try and produce a scoring chance nearer to goal.

(b) Dribble in order to produce a scoring chance nearer to goal.

(c) Shoot for goal.

Situations and players vary of course. When the penalty area is crowded, however, there will be a greater percentage success ratio for shooting than for either dribbling or inter-passing.

Attacking the opposition without the ball

There are two primary objectives in moving forward to attack opponents without the ball.

(1) To take defenders out of good positions and into poor defending positions

Two important points to remember are these. First, defenders will often wish to retreat towards their own goal in order to consolidate their defence by reducing both angles and spaces in a vital area of the field. Attackers, therefore, should endeavour to attack on as wide a front as possible and try to take defenders also wide away from central defending positions and out of their normal line of retreat.

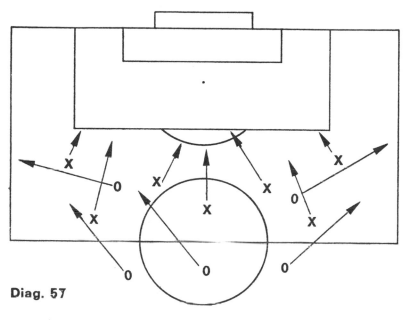

Diag. 57

In diagram 57 the X players are shown in their normal and accepted lines of retreat. The O team must try and make the opposite type of run in order to stop one or more X player from retreating and possibly pull them wide away from central retreating positions.

Secondly, defenders will wish to support each other. Attackers, therefore, should attack supporting players by running at them and past them in order to take the supporting players into positions where support is not possible.

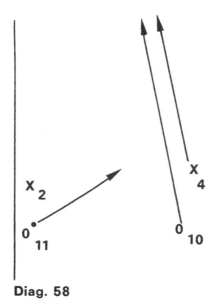

Diag. 58

In diagram 58 X_2 is supported by X_4. But X_4 is attacked by O_{10} without the ball and X_4 is taken into a position from which he cannot support X_2. O_{11} therefore, with the ball, takes advantage of the space by attacking X_2 by dribbling past him on the inside.

In diagram 59 X_6 is supporting X_3. But O_8 runs past O_7 and attracts X_6 by taking him into a position from which he cannot support X_3. O_7, therefore, takes advantage of the space and attacks X_3 by dribbling past him on the outside and then moving inside.

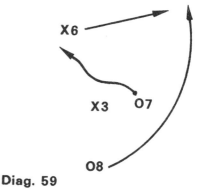

Diag. 59

(2) Running into the space beyond opponents in order that the player with the ball has the opportunity to pass the ball past opponents into the space behind them

This point was mentioned in the previous chapter and it is of such importance that it is worth emphasising again now. Defenders are not troubled by opponents who play in front of them. They are not greatly concerned by opponents who move level with them. But every good defender knows the effects of allowing an opponent to move into a position behind him could be disastrous.

Curved or 'bent' runs can be most effective for attackers in assisting them to get past opponents on the blind side.

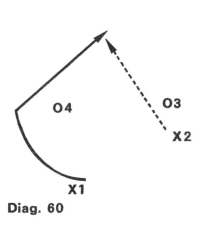

Diag. 60

In diagram 60 X_1 has made a curved run to take advantage of O_4 who is watching the ball to the exclusion of the player X_1. Note that X_1 when on the blind side of O_4 and almost level with him accelerates and, therefore, straightens his run to move into the space behind O_4 and receives the ball from X_2. This is a most effective type of run and is used with most telling effect by several world class players. None is better at this type of run, however, than Martin Peters of England.

CONCLUSION AND SUMMARY

Successful team-work requires that players attack opponents with and without the ball. It is necessary to stress again that what players can do as individuals is important but it is what players do as a team that really counts.

Try and remember the following points :—

(1) Attack opponents by passing the ball forward. Remember the four principles of good passing.
(2) Attack opponents by dribbling the ball past them. Remember the two important points in dribbling.
(3) Attack opponents by shooting the ball past them.
(4) Attack opponents without the ball—taking defenders into poor defending positions.
(5) Attack opponents without the ball by running into the space behind them.

CHAPTER 8

THE DO'S AND DON'TS OF PASSING

Nothing destroys a team quite so quickly as inaccurate passing. Nothing builds a team's confidence more rapidly than good accurate passing. Without good team-work accurate passing is impossible. With good team-work accurate passing becomes much simplified. The more successful passes a player makes the better he is likely to play and the more he is likely to want to play. The art of passing in Association Football is very largely the art of doing the simple things quickly and well.

Move to meet the pass

A large number of passes are intercepted by defenders who take advantage of attackers who wait for the ball to reach them. Attackers should move to meet the pass—this is particularly true in the defending and middle thirds of the field.

Moving into the line of the pass

It is important that players in positions in advance of the ball should present easy targets by moving into positions between defenders and then into the line of the pass.

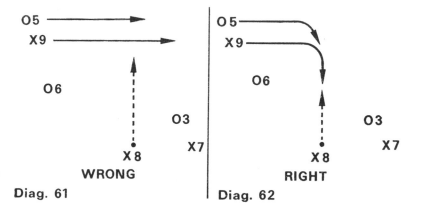

Diag. 61   WRONG

Diag. 62   RIGHT

In diagram 61 X_9 has run across the field and given X_8 the impossible task of firing at a moving target. This is wrong.

In diagram 62 X_9 has played much better and has moved into a space behind and in between O_6 and O_3. Having achieved this position X_9 turns to move into the line of the pass. This makes the passing of the ball very much easier for X_8 and is good and correct play by X_9.

When to pass the ball forward and when to pass the ball backwards

If a player can pass the ball forward he should do so. But to pass the ball forward he needs two things. First, space in front of his opponent. Second, a team-mate to pass to.

If the player with the ball is pressurised and cannot pass the ball forward he needs support from behind, and he should pass the ball backwards to his supporting player. One of the reasons why teams are poor at supporting in attack is that players, who are in no position to pass the ball forward, refuse to pass the ball backwards. Indeed some coaches try and insist that the ball is not played backwards. If this attitude prevails there is no point whatever, or any likelihood of employment, for the player who supports from behind the ball.

The fact of the matter is, of course, that if a player cannot pass the ball forward, the quicker he realises this, and changes the point of attack by passing the ball to a player who is in a position to pass the ball forward, the better.

The converse is also true, however. If a player is in a position to pass the ball forward and fails to do so he has played badly. In modern football, principally because there is a tendency to play more players in mid-field positions, there is likewise a tendency to pass the ball across the field rather than forwards towards one's opponent's goal. If the mid-field area is flooded with opponents it is more important than ever to take every opportunity of playing the ball past them.

Passing through the defending and the middle thirds of the field to be consistently effective requires three essential ingredients:—

(1) It needs to be accurate.
(2) It needs to be simple.
(3) It needs to be quick.

(1) Accuracy

In order to be accurate it is helpful to aim most of the passes to feet. This not only helps the players to play more quickly but in tight situations it gives the defenders the least chance of winning the ball. Furthermore, passes placed in front of players into space often require a judgment of pace which is not easy to achieve. Passes to feet, therefore, will pay the biggest dividends in the defending and middle thirds of the field. That is not to say that no effective passes in these areas will ever be played to space. It is to say that something of the order of 90% of passes should be played to feet.

Simple passes

It is, I think, a characteristic of the amateur player in all games that he strives manfully to achieve the difficult and the spectacular. So it is that the amateur bowler in cricket tries to bowl too fast and succeeds only in losing length and direction. The park tennis player spends his time on court trying to serve aces and hit winners off every stroke. No long rallies for him. It's all or nothing on every shot. The fact that it usually turns out to be nothing never seems to persuade these players to consider if there is not a more effective method of playing. Golf, it should be pointed out, is an exception amongst all games for the real amateur, in as much that the worse one plays the more hits one gets at the ball !

In football some players live their lives trying to hit defence splitting passes from positions where the defence is secure. One should understand why players do this. There are two fundamental reasons.

In the first place they do not understand just how inefficient they are. It goes almost without saying that they do not know what they could do which would be more efficient.

In the second place they make this sort of mistake because they become impatient. Once a player becomes impatient he takes uncalculated risks, and thereby he takes the first step towards being inefficient and reducing his part in the game to a lottery.

Simple passes will usually pay the biggest dividends in the defending and middle thirds of the field and certainly patience will always be rewarded.

Quick passes

Quick passing does not only mean one touch passing—two and three touches are also quick. But it does mean playing with the head up looking for passing opportunities. It does mean also frequent changes in the point of attack.

Every team should practise one touch football. Not only will this prove the best means of speeding up the passing of the ball, but it will also make players assess situations before they receive the ball rather than after they have received the ball. It also encourages players to move into supporting positions quickly. It should be understood that there is a vast difference between one touch and two touch football. Two touch football allows the player to receive the ball before he looks up to assess the situation. This is one of the causes of slow play. To play at a high level, against opponents who pressurise consistently, a team must be capable of playing accurate one touch football.

One often hears people say 'make the ball do the work'. What these people are usually asking for is the ball being played more quickly. They are absolutely right. Quick play is an essential quality in effective team-work and teams will neglect this quality at their peril.

The importance of disguise

This quality has been mentioned in previous chapters. Suffice it here to reiterate that the ability to disguise one's intentions is one of the characteristics of an outstanding player in Association Football. It is a means of relieving pressure by creating space or time. It also makes opponents move into false positions.

Where to try the difficult and when to calculate on the side of risk

The attacking third of the field is the area of the field where attackers must calculate on the side of risk in their passing and go for passes through difficult angles and into small spaces. Effective passing in the attacking third of the field requires three things :—
(1) Good technique.
(2) Good judgment.
(3) Confidence.

(1) Good technique

Good technique involves the qualities of passing discussed in Chapter Seven. It also involves a wide range of techniques. If a player cannot bend the ball round opponents, or chip the ball over the top of them, then clearly his range of techniques is limited, and his effectiveness will be limited in the attacking third of the field.

The way in which modern strategy has developed, and will continue to develop in the next few years, will cause greater emphasis to be placed on techniques of passing the ball, and especially passing the ball in the attacking third of the field.

(2) Good judgment

Judgment of passing possibilities in the attacking third of the field requires an acute awareness of angles and distances, an awareness too of the capabilities of one's own players and the inadequacies of one's opponents. Good judgment in passing is not developed by divine right, it is developed by realistic practice, and plenty of it.

(3) Confidence

Confidence in passing is developed by the knowledge of two factors. First, the knowledge of what is required and what constitutes an acceptable percentage of success and, secondly, knowledge of what you can do as a technician. Confidence is put to the test, not when players are playing well, but rather when players are inaccurate in situations when they would normally expect to be accurate. What it amounts to is this: we all make mistakes but some can rise above their mistakes better than others. That is what confidence is about. It is part of the task of Managers and Coaches to help players up off the floor to rise above their mistakes.

The don'ts of passing

There are four major don'ts which it is helpful to remember. They are :—
(1) Don't run with the ball.
(2) Don't pass the ball square across the field.
(3) Don't play long optimistic inaccurate passes.
(4) Don't present a numerical advantage to the opposition.

(1) Don't run with the ball

Running with the ball should be avoided as a general rule in the defending and middle thirds of the field. The tendency is for the player running with the ball to run into trouble. It is also a tendency for players running with the ball to do so with their heads down, and team-mates in good positions to receive a pass are not observed. Running with the ball also leads to slow play. It should also be remembered that it is much harder physically to run with the ball than it is to run without the ball. In the end fatigue makes every player less efficient. Players who persist in running with the ball advance the stage at which fatigue sets in and they become less efficient.

It is worth noting that as players become fatigued the tendency is to run with the ball more—not less.

Suffice it to say that if players persist in running with the ball in the defending and middle-thirds of the field, they will succeed only in playing for the opposition.

Attacking opponents by dribbling past them in the attacking third of the field is a different matter altogether, and is an important factor in efficient team performance. This has been dealt with in Chapter Seven.

(2) Don't pass the ball square across the field

Balls which are passed square across the field involve a colossal element of risk. The risk is that the ball will be intercepted and a minimum of two players put immediately out of the game. The risk is greatest in the defending third of the field. Experienced players can and do pass the ball square to good effect but one has so often seen even experienced players miscalculate. If players never played a square pass one can hardly imagine that their game would suffer greatly because of it. If players, on the other hand, miscalculate when passing the ball square, then it is more than likely that the team will suffer and possibly lose a goal.

(3) Don't play long optimistic inaccurate passes

Long optimistic inaccurate passes also put players out of the game. It is usual that a present of space is made to the opposition since the attacking team is invariably stretched end to end. There is nothing wrong with long passes if they are accurate. But so often the intention is incorrect.

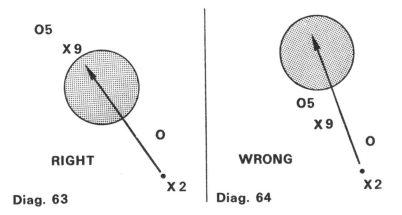

Diag. 63   Diag. 64

In diagram 63 X_2 has played the ball into the space in front of X_9. This is the correct pass for X_9 to receive in this situation.

In diagram 64 X_2 has played the ball into the space beyond X_9 and behind O_5. O_5 will be first to the ball. Furthermore the X team will be stretched at a time when, having lost the ball, they require to be compact. That obviously is wrong.

(4) Don't present a numerical advantage to the opposition

Reference has been made in this book to the importance of concentration. Players are likely to lose their concentration on three occasions :—

(a) When they are fatigued.

(b) When the ball changes hands.

(c) When the game stops.

It is on all the above three occasions that a team is likely to present the opposition with a numerical advantage.

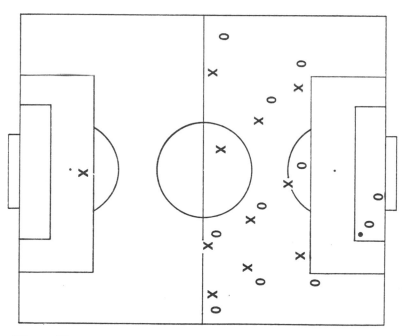

Diag. 65

There are other occasions too when a team may present the opposition with a numerical advantage. A player, for example, who fails to tie up his boot-lace properly is likely to put himself out of the game for thirty seconds or more. If players have trouble with boot-laces which come undone they should follow the scout motto and be prepared—tie a reef knot.

Players who go to ground unnecessarily, e.g. sliding tackle, may present the opposition with a numerical advantage.

So too does the goalkeeper who cannot, or will not, take his own goal-kicks.

In diagram 65 the O team is taking a goal-kick. There are two O players inside the six yard area because the O goalkeeper will not take the kick.

Since the ball must travel outside the penalty area from a goal kick the O team is committed to play the ball into an area of the field where they are outnumbered 10 v 9.

CONCLUSION AND SUMMARY

All good teams are good passers of the ball and good passing depends as much on team-work as it does on individual technique. Good teams appreciate one thing above all else concerning the passing of the ball: in which area of the field to calculate on the side of safety and where to calculate on the side of risk.

Try and remember the following key points :—

(1) Move to meet the pass and move into the line of the pass.
(2) When to pass the ball forward and when to pass the ball back.
(3) Play to feet especially in the defending and middle thirds of the field.
(4) Simple play is the most effective.
(5) Play the ball quickly.
(6) The importance of disguise.
(7) Where to try the difficult and where to calculate on the side of risk.
(8) The Don'ts of passing :—
    (a) Don't run with the ball.
    (b) Don't pass the ball square across the field.
    (c) Don't play long optimistic inaccurate passes.
    (d) Don't present a numerical advantage to the opposition.

CHAPTER 9

SHOOTING

Shooting is not only the most exciting part of Association Football it is also the most important part of attacking play. Too often we are satisfied with having created scoring opportunities and not sufficiently dissatisfied with our inability to convert chances into goals.

Missed opportunities

It is a fact, that at every level of football a high percentage of opportunities to shoot are missed ; by that one means that the shot is never taken. The number of goals scored would rapidly increase if all players shot for goal on every occasion when they had an opportunity to shoot.

Some consider it one of the mysteries of life as to why players don't shoot when they are in a position to do so. There is no mystery about it. Some teachers and coaches are to blame, in the first place, for encouraging and praising players for their unselfish play. Where scoring goals is concerned unselfish players do not win matches. It should be understood that players who are praised, when they pass the responsibility for shooting, for that on most occasions is what unselfish play is, will continue to be irresponsible and will continue to lack aggression in their finishing. Players in shooting positions should accept their responsibility. That responsibility is not only for scoring but also for missing—one cannot have it both ways. The facts on the percentages are, that a player will miss many more times than he will score.

Crowds too can adversely affect players in their shooting. The player who scores is a hero and the one who misses is a mug. We all know that that player is often one and the same man in one and the same match. To miss the goal with a shot is, of course, a mistake, even hitting the crossbar or a post is a mistake since no player ever aims for the woodwork. But players should understand, and coaches should encourage players to appreciate, that the biggest mistake of all is not to take a shot for goal when in a position to do so.

Shots off target

It is also a fact that a high percentage of shots which are taken miss the target. These are shots which do not even require the goalkeeper to make a save. Accuracy in shooting should be emphasised before an emphasis is placed on power. Players, when shooting, frequently go berserk and concentrate only upon power. This is power out of control, and power out of control means inaccuracy.

All players, but more especially young players, like to see the net bulge. But they must see even more clearly the means whereby to make it bulge.

Accuracy, therefore, is the top priority in teaching players to shoot.

The importance of low shots

Shots which are on the ground are more difficult for a goalkeeper to save than shots which are in the air. One realises that shots along the ground look less spectacular than shots which hit the roof of the net. The fact remains that shots which are in the air are usually easier for a goalkeeper to reach than shots along the ground.

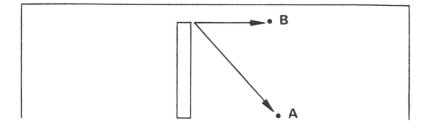

Diag. 66

Diagram 66 shows that a goalkeeper will move quicker to a ball at point B than he will to a ball at point A. Point A is actually further away than point B when one considers that the goalkeeper has to move the whole of his body to save at point A. At point B it may be possible to save by stretching out one arm.

Furthermore it is easier to assess the flight of balls in the air—these balls are not subject to deviation unless they hit a player en route. Shots along the ground, however, are likely to bump, skid or stick, all of which make the stopping of the shot a little more difficult.

The importance of shots going away from the goalkeeper

Shots going away from the goalkeeper, that is shots to the far post, are usually more difficult to save than shots coming into the goalkeeper, that is shots at the near post.

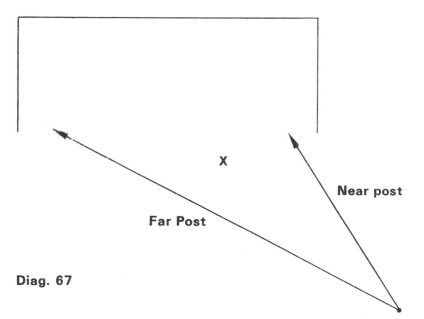

X

Near post

Far Post

Diag. 67

Not only is it more difficult to reach shots to the far post but, because the ball is going away from the goalkeeper, the ball is more difficult to hold even if the goalkeeper reaches it.

Aston Villa skipper Dennis Mortimer is chased by West Bromwich Albion's Tony Brown (left) as he shoots past Albion skipper John Wile (5).

TACTICS AND TEAMWORK

The value of swerving and power shots

The job of a goalkeeper is to hold shots which are fired at his goal. The job of attacking players is to make it as difficult as possible for the goalkeeper to hold the ball. Swerving shots and powerful shots are difficult for goalkeepers to hold and secondary scoring chances or 'knock downs' frequently occur from these shots.

The flight of these type of shots, particularly swerving shots, is difficult to judge and especially if the ball is shot past many players.

Far too few shots are taken from outside the penalty area. With more and more players being withdrawn into deep defensive positions it is becoming more and more important for attacking players to develop the technique of shooting for goal from twenty-five and thirty yards range. There is advantage in doing so. If many players are positioned in front of the goal the goal-keeper may be unsighted or there may be a deflection. The chances of one or other of these possibilities must always be quite good when the penalty area is crowded with players. The alternatives to shooting in these situations are twofold. One is to interpass to create a scoring chance nearer to goal; the other alternative is to dribble the ball to create a scoring chance. If players play the percentages on these three possibilities they will be encouraged to take more shots from twenty-five and thirty yards range.

The frequency of bouncing or dropping balls in the penalty area

A high percentage of scoring chances inevitably occur from dropping or bouncing balls in and around the penalty area. These chances invariably fall into the half-chance category. But it is half-chances that often win matches. Players need frequent practice at taking this type of shot and they need to develop the ability to adjust their bodies quickly to unusual shooting positions.

Approximately 50% of opportunities to shoot are from dropping or bouncing balls. Approximately 90% of shooting practices are with rolling balls.

Mention has been made of the fact that more and more players seem to be appearing in defensive positions. In consequence, the ground route to goal is becoming more difficult to expose. On many occasions there is no alternative but to pass the ball over the heads of defenders. This inevitably means that the attacker receiving the ball must strike a falling or bouncing ball. Set plays have assumed a much greater importance over the last few years but here again the service almost invariably requires that the striker has to deal with a falling or bouncing ball.

England striker Bob Latchford dives in at the near post to head England's first goal past Wales' Dai Davies.

TACTICS AND TEAMWORK

There is one simple but tremendously important technical point for players to remember when kicking a falling or bouncing ball into the goal:

The ball must be struck through the top half to keep the ball down.

If a player strikes the ball through the bottom half the ball will rise.

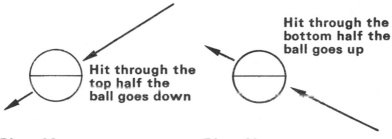

Hit through the bottom half the ball goes up

Hit through the top half the ball goes down

Diag. 68   **Diag. 69**

There is no need to delve into body mechanics to establish why a ball went over the bar. The ball went over the bar because the ball was hit through the bottom half and one does not need to have seen the shot to establish that fact.

It has not been one of the objectives of this book to write in any detail about technique analysis. But this is a suitable juncture to make the point that many teachers and coaches complicate the teaching, and therefore the learning, of techniques. We would all do well to remember, both in relation to tactics and techniques, that that which is complicated will not work and that which is effective is also simple and easy to understand. If that is not so then Association Football is not a game for simple folk. The fact is, however, that a large number of simple folk play Association Football particularly well.

Forwards should practise keeping the ball down and they should practise both volleys and half-volleys from both falling and bouncing balls. Perhaps one should explain the reason for practising with both falling and bouncing balls. The reason, which will be readily appreciated, is that there is a difference between striking a ball which is falling and striking a ball which is rising. Bouncing balls often have to be hit whilst the ball is rising. These are the shots which are the most difficult to keep down.

England's Kevin Keegan heads the ball from the near post back to a team-mate (Bob Latchford) at the far post.

The importance of quickness

Quickness of thought and quickness of action are invaluable assets for forward players, especially in and around the penalty area. This quality can be trained. A practice which will prove helpful is to have a group of players in an area twenty-four yards by eighteen yards, i.e. the width of the six yard area and the distance from the goal-line to the edge of the penalty area.

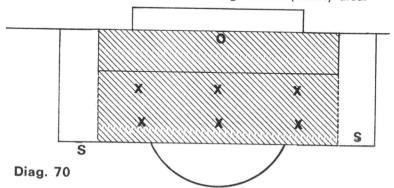

Diag. 70

In diagram 70 the shaded area contains six X players and O is the goalkeeper. The two servers (S) each require a good supply of footballs, and the balls are served into the shaded area one at a time. When the ball goes out of the shaded area another ball is served in immediately. When any X player receives the ball, or takes possession of the ball, he attacks the goal. When any X player is not in possession of the ball he defends against the player who is in possession. The situation, therefore, is always 1 v 5. The practice is fairly intense and should last not more than one minute. It is, of course, possible to vary the practice by having more or fewer players and also by arranging the players in teams, i.e. 3 v 3 or 4 v 4 rather than 1 v 5.

However, the major points are, that the space should be restricted in order that the players should have little time and space in which to take their shots; the players should always be under challenge, and the service should be as varied as possible.

The importance of composure

Players must try and develop an awareness in their shooting, an awareness that is, of time and space and the position of opponents, especially the goalkeeper. An awareness too of when to set a premium on power and when to set a premium on clinical accuracy.

It is important that players play with their heads up in order to assess the situation. Sometimes a player will find himself clear of the defence with only the goalkeeper to beat. These chances look easy—they never are. One or two points, however, might prove helpful:

    (a) The chip over the goalkeeper's head is a most difficult technique because the ball is invariably rolling away from the kicker.

    (b) If the player decides to dribble round the goalkeeper he must make sure that the ball is played past the goalkeeper, not to the side of him.

    (c) If the goalkeeper is moving out from his goal very quickly a shot even within inches of the goalkeeper will be very difficult to save since it will be impossible for the goalkeeper to change direction.

    (d) Shots on the ground will have the best chance of scoring.

    (e) Shots on the ground and to the far post will have the best chance of all.

It is most important, in all shooting situations, but more especially when a player is clear of the defence, with only the goalkeeper to beat, that a player should keep his composure when all about him might well be losing theirs.

CONCLUSION AND SUMMARY

Of all the skills in Association Football which require constant practice, shooting is the most important; of all the skills in Association Football which are deficient, shooting is the most glaring example; of all the key factors in Association Football none is more important than shooting.

Try and remember the following points:—

    (1) Many opportunities to shoot are missed, i.e. the shot is never taken.

    (2) A high percentage of shots miss the target—go for accuracy before power.

    (3) Low shots are better than high shots.

    (4) Shots to the far post are more difficult to save than shots to the near post.

    (5) Swerving and powerful shots are valuable.

    (6) 50% of shooting chances come from falling or bouncing balls.

    (7) Balls which are hit through the bottom half will go up: balls which are hit through the top half will go down.

    (8) The importance of quickness.

    (9) The importance of composure.

CHAPTER 10

DEFENDING AT SET PLAYS

It is difficult to defend at set plays for two particular reasons. First, the opposition can place large numbers of attacking players in pre-planned attacking positions. Second, it is impossible to exert a high degree of pressure on the service since, with the exception of a throw-in, the defending players always have to be ten yards away from the ball.

It is a fact that 40% of goals are scored from set plays, and the moral behind that fact is that defence at set plays requires the most careful planning, organisation and concentration. The basic problem is twofold :—

(1) Marking players.

(2) Marking space.

We shall consider now how best to defend at free kicks, corners and throwing in.

Free kicks

Wherever a free kick is conceded a player should be detailed to adopt a position ten yards away from the ball in a direct line between the ball and his own goal. By adopting this position he achieves three possible objectives.

(1) He is on the goal-side of the ball and in a position to move forward and challenge for the ball if a short free kick is taken.

(2) It is possible that the kicker will direct his kick away from the direct line to goal, which is the line in which the defender is standing.

(3) If the kicker aims the ball along the direct line to goal it will be necessary to play the ball over the head of the defender thus producing a more difficult ball for his team-mates to receive.

If the defender moves his position slightly as the kicker approaches the ball, it is possible that this will induce some inaccuracy in the kick.

The defending third of the field

In the defending third of the field and particularly around the penalty area it will be necessary to erect a wall to seal off part of the goal.

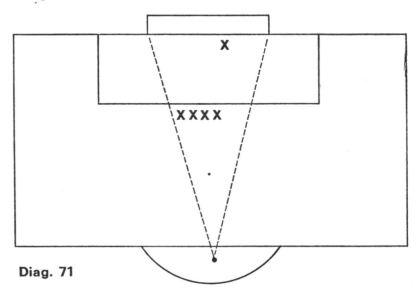

Diag. 71

It is vital that the wall should be placed in position ten yards away from the ball, not only because that is the law but because there are great risks if the wall is set five yards from the ball and then moved back by the referee.

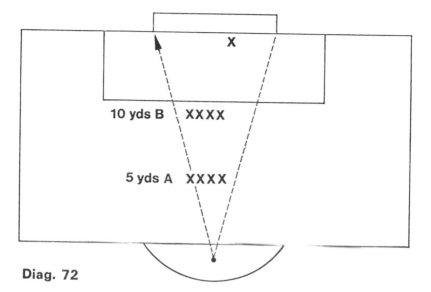

Diag. 72

In diagram 72 it is clear that at point A four players will seal off more of the goal than at point B. At point B a team would be extremely vulnerable to a direct shot.

Furthermore, by placing the wall at point A, the goalkeeper will have to move further across his goal in order to see the ball. This makes him rather vulnerable to a ball chipped over the wall.

Setting the wall

The wall should be set in position by an out player rather than the goalkeeper. A goalkeeper setting the wall has to move to a post in order to line up the wall, and in so doing leaves the whole of his goal open.

England line up to face a free-kick as Scotland's Don Masson plays the ball square.

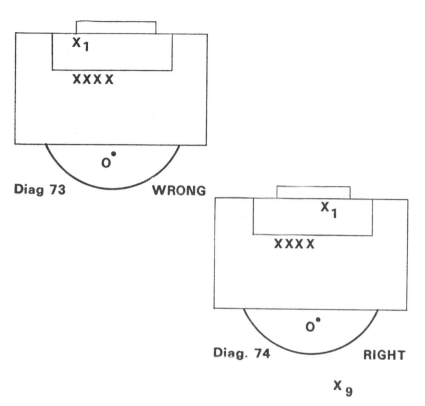

Diag 73   WRONG

Diag. 74   RIGHT

In diagram 73 it can be seen that X_1, the goalkeeper, who is setting the wall, is in no position to defend his goal.

In diagram 74 the wall is being set by X_9 and X_1 is in a good position to defend his goal.

It should be understood that the duty of the goalkeeper is to defend his goal and he should be relieved of all other responsibilities which will prevent his doing that duty.

The outplayer setting the wall need only position one man between the ball and the post. His job is then done and he can concentrate upon taking up his defensive position. If four players are required in the wall two will line up on the inside of the player in line with the post, and one will line up on the outside of the player in line with the post. It is absolutely vital that one player should block off space outside the line between the ball and the post in order to prevent the bent shot round the outside of the wall.

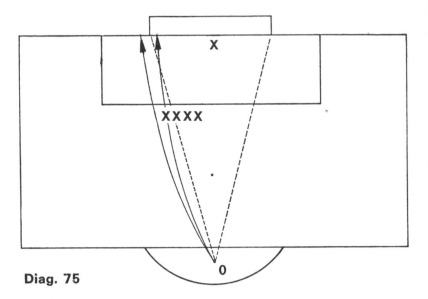

Diag. 75

Diagram 75 shows the position of one defending player outside the line between the ball and the post. It also shows what is likely to happen if a player is not placed in that position.

The position of the goalkeeper

The position of the goalkeeper should be to the side of the wall, not behind the wall, but not so far to the side of the wall to make him vulnerable to the bent shot round the inside of the wall or over the wall.

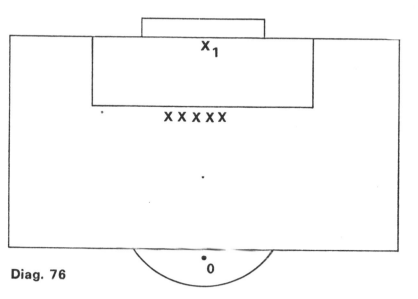

Diag. 76

In diagram 76 X_1, the goalkeeper, is positioned behind the wall in a position from which he will have difficulty in sighting the ball. Although the goalkeeper is in a central position the fact that he cannot see the ball makes his position incorrect. This, of course, is the dilemma which goalkeepers face when they also want a large number of players in the wall: five or six players in a wall can seal off more than half of the goal but it leaves the goalkeeper with two difficult choices:

(a) He can move to one side of his goal from which he will have a good view of the ball but will be vulnerable to a chip shot to his far post.

(b) He can adopt a central position behind his wall and settle for the fact that he will see the ball late.

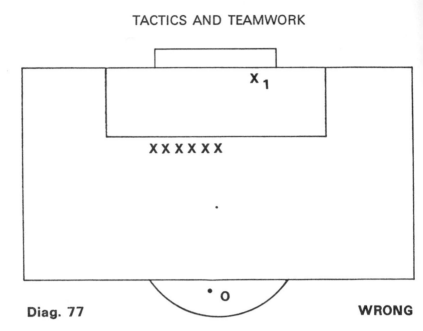

Diag. 77   **WRONG**

In diagram 77 there are six players in the wall and X_1, the goal-keeper, has found it necessary to move to one side of his goal in order to get a satisfactory view of the ball. The goalkeeper's view may be satisfactory but his position is far from satisfactory.

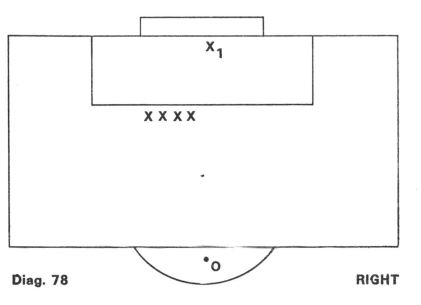

Diag. 78   **RIGHT**

In diagram 78 X_1 is in a position which is almost central in his goal. That is correct. A goalkeeper who is more than one yard away from the centre of his goal can consider his position to be less than satisfactory.

How many players in a wall?

The answer to this question very largely depends on the position of the ball. It should, however, be appreciated that it is a mistake to lock up too many players in the wall since opponents in dangerous positions must be marked. If a team places six players in a wall they are gambling on the opposition not sending large numbers of players forward into the danger zone. In these circumstances, excluding the goalkeepers, the potential situation away from the wall is four defenders v nine attackers. That is a bad risk by any standard.

What then is the correct number of players to place in a wall? A rough guide (see diagram 79) is as follows:—

(a) In the 'D', four or five players.

(b) To the side of the 'D', three or four players.

(c) To the side of the penalty area, two or three players.

99

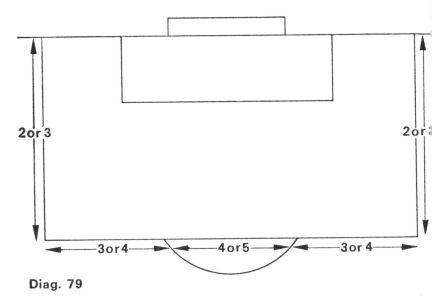

Diag. 79

As the position of the kick moves out towards the touch-lines then obviously the number of players required in the wall decreases, eventually down to one. And the same thing happens as the position of the kick is moved back from the edge of the penalty area towards the half-way line.

The only occasion when it would be acceptable, therefore, to have a wall with more than five players in it, is when an indirect free kick is awarded inside the penalty area probably less than ten yards from goal. In these circumstances it is best to withdraw all players into defending positions and make one wall of eleven players.

Before we finish on the question of walls one more point should be made. Players in a wall sometimes link arms or hold each other round the waist. This is not a good idea since players should be as free as possible to move away from the wall once the kick has been taken. Players, in order to give themselves some protection against a ball driven at them, should cross their hands in front of their lower abdomen and slightly bow their heads in order that the ball cannot hit them in the face.

Sealing off vital space

The point has been made that it is a mistake to lock up too many players in the wall. It is also a mistake to lock up your best defending players.

If a free kick is in the 'D' then the whole team must defend and should be exclusively concerned with the area between the six yard area and the edge of the penalty area—roughly 24 yards by 12 yards. Since there is a possibility that the angle of the shot will be changed by a short pass for a second player to shoot, it is vital for two players to threaten the kick. In diagram 80 these two players are X_9 and X_{10}.

As the ball is moved to the side of the 'D' so the direct threat on the goal decreases but the vital space to seal off increases. In diagram 81 the positions are shown for the defending players against a free kick from the side of the 'D'. It is important to note the positions of two players.

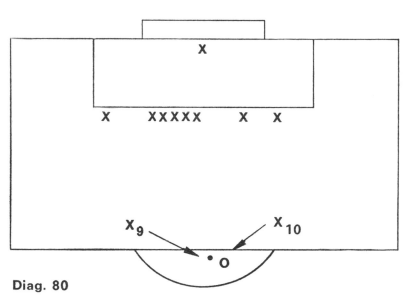

Diag. 80

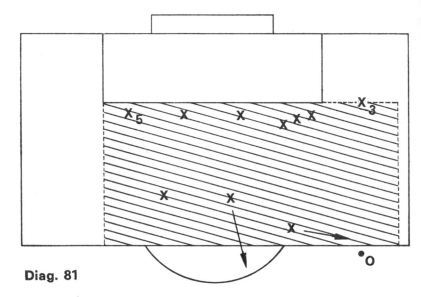

Diag. 81

X_3 is the left full-back positioned to meet the threat to the outside of the wall where he would have to defend as a left full-back. He should be the best player in the team to defend that space.

X_5 is positioned outside the far post to deal with the high cross. It is important that this player is a good header of the ball and this position is usually best occupied by the centre-half.

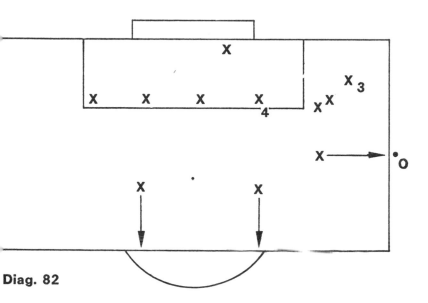

Diag. 82

As the position of the ball is moved down the side of the penalty area still more space has to be sealed off. Please note in diagram 82 that X_3 still defends the outside of the wall. But the most important position of all is X_4. From all flank free kicks from just outside the penalty area and even much further out from goal the threat to the near post is enormous. The position of X_4, therefore, is roughly in a line between the ball and the far post and almost level with the near post.

Defence at corners

Exactly the same principles apply to defence at corners as at free kicks.

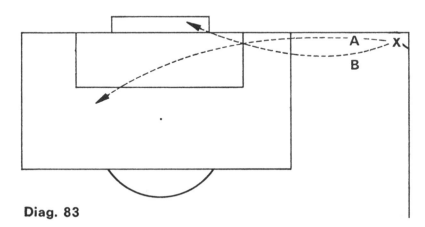

Diag. 83

It is advisable to detail a player to threaten the kick from a distance of ten yards. There are two reasons for this. The first reason is to disturb the kicker. Diagram 83 shows that there are two possible positions for the player threatening the kick, depending on whether the kick is an out-swinger or an in-swinger. The job of the player threatening the kick is to threaten the line of flight. This he will best achieve by moving into the line of flight just as the player taking the kick approaches the ball.

If the kick is an out-swinger then he will position near to the goal-line in position A.

If the kick is an in-swinger then he will position further out from the goal-line in position B.

The second reason for sending a player to threaten the kick is to have one player already in position should the opposition decide to take a short corner.

Short corners

There is usually no problem in dealing with short corners provided the defending team has equal numbers with the attackers in the area of the ball. It is important, therefore, that if the opposition places two players in the area of the corner, the defending team should send a second player to support the player who will already be in position to threaten the kick.

Care should be taken to ensure that a tall player is not drawn out of the middle at short corners. Tall players should retain central positions in order to retain dominance in the air.

The position of the goalkeeper

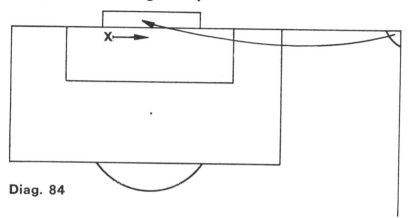

Diag. 84

Almost from time immemorial goalkeepers have gone to the far post to position for corners. With modern strategy and techniques for taking corner kicks this is a mistake. The goalkeeper requires to take up a position at least half way across his goal and possibly even in the front half of his goal. The problem is twofold :—

    (a) The time factor in getting across the goal to deal with a fast driven in-spinning ball.

    (b) The physical problem (see diagram 85) of getting across the goal through a densely populated area. It cannot be done.

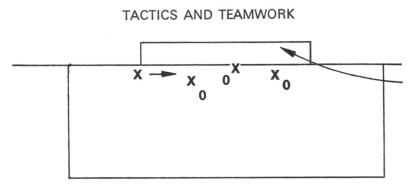

Diag. 85

The position of the full-backs

Full-backs frequently position themselves at corner kicks inside the goal and watch the kick through the side-netting. It is common to see full-backs position inside the post on the goal-line.

From a position on the goal-line full-backs can only defend a space along the goal-line. It is preferable that full-backs should position slightly outside the posts and slightly in-field as indicated in diagram 86.

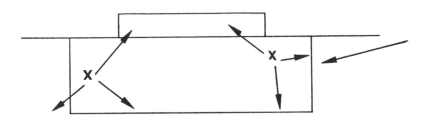

Diag. 86

From these positions they can seal off more space and still do their job on the goal-line if necessary. The full-back on the far post can position slightly further out because he has slightly more time.

Defending the near post

This is without question the area where most problems develop against the modern corner kick, particularly the in-swinger.

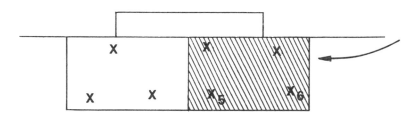

Diag. 87

Diagram 87 shows the vital area of the front half of the six yard area.

Players should be carefully selected for positions X_5 and X_6. They should, of course, be good headers of the ball, but most of all they should be good at attacking the ball—that is moving towards the ball to beat the opponents to the ball.

Defending the far post

In their enthusiasm to defend the near post a team must not assume that they are not vulnerable at the far post. They must ensure that they are not vulnerable, and this they can only do by having players there.

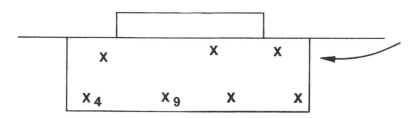

Diag. 88

Once again it is helpful if the full-back comes off his line and seals off some space. It is also helpful if the centre-forward, X_9, is a good defensive header of the ball.

These players should not need to adjust their positions to any great extent to deal with opponents if the goalkeeper is prepared to deal with any opponent who positions himself on the goal-line, particularly in the front half of the goal.

Defending the area between the 6 yard and the 18 yard lines

Because the six yard area is likely to be so heavily populated, and because defenders are likely to have to play the ball against the spin, the ball will be difficult to clear. Further, one must not assume that the ball will always be played into the six yard area. It is important, therefore, that the area between the six yard area and the edge of the penalty area should be well defended.

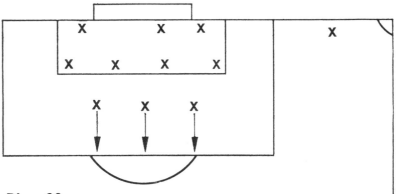

Diag. 89

Diagram 89 shows the complete arrangement of all eleven players.

Adjustments will be necessary to these positions if, for example, a player or players, have to move out to deal with a short corner. But it is a sound basic structure for defence at corners.

Some may prefer to leave one player, or more than one player, in an advanced position on the half-way line. This is a matter of choice. Remember this, however. Having conceded a corner the first task is to clear the danger.

Defending at throws

At most throws defensive problems are caused by players being left un-marked—particularly the thrower.

The root cause of the problem is lack of concentration. Players do not seem to be aware of how many goals are scored from throws.

Concentration

Players should concentrate on marking tight and pressurising players in the area of the ball; and the time to pick up the marking is while the ball is being retrieved.

Attacking players will try and take quick throws—the antidote is quick tight marking. Remember the player receiving the ball has to control or pass a dropping ball and it will be difficult to maintain control under effective pressure.

Long throws in the attacking third of the field

Modern strategy combined with good throwing techniques is causing more and more problems from throws in the attacking third of the field. The player receiving the throw should be challenged from in front as well as from behind and as much space inside the penalty area as possible should be sealed off. (See diagram 90).

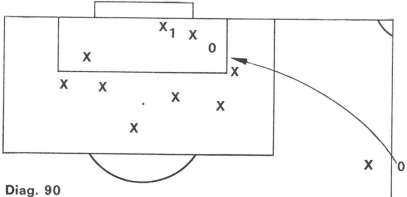

Diag. 90

Please note in diagram 90 that X_1, the goalkeeper, has moved into the front half of his goal to defend against the throw. There must be no question of the goalkeeper taking up a position at the far post.

CONCLUSION AND SUMMARY

Defensive organisation at set plays need to be thought out in detail. It is important that players should be detailed to specific tasks and each defence rehearsed. When players know what task they have to perform they concentrate upon doing it. If every player concentrates 100% in his task the danger from set plays is immediately reduced considerably.

Try and remember the following points :—

(1) Free kicks :—
    (a) Threaten the kick.
    (b) Setting the wall.
    (c) The position of the goalkeeper.
    (d) Don't put too many players in the wall.
    (e) Sealing off vital space.

(2) Corners :—
    (a) How to threaten the kick.
    (b) How to defend against short corners.
    (c) The position of the goalkeeper.
    (d) The position of the full-backs.
    (e) Defending the near post.
    (f) Defending the far post.
    (g) Defending the space between the six yard line and the eighteen yard line.

(3) Throw in :—
    (a) The importance of concentration.
    (b) Mark tight in the area of the ball including the thrower.
    (c) At long throws mark the receiver from in-front and from behind.

CHAPTER 11

ATTACKING AT SET PLAYS

In Chapter Ten the case was stated for the importance of set plays to be recognised more fully. It is a fact that 40% of goals are scored from set plays and that fact tells its own story. But it is also a fact that vital matches are often decided by a free kick, a corner or a throw-in. In the World Cup series of 1966 England's vital quarter-final match against Argentina was won from a throw-in. In the Final of the same series England equalised West Germany's early goal through a free kick and took a 2-1 lead through a corner. West Germany's remarkable equaliser, on the stroke of full-time, came from a free kick. It is now history that the World Cup Final of 1966 ended 4-2 in England's favour but remember 50% of these goals were scored from set plays. Set plays were, therefore, important in 1966, and they are of even greater importance now. Teams will overlook and underestimate the importance of set plays at their peril and it is worth remembering that, in tight defensive matches, it is set plays which frequently offer a team its best chance of scoring goals.

It is, of course, quite understandable why set plays should be so dangerous. When, in modern football, is a player allowed to kick a dead ball with no opponent within ten yards of him, other than at a set play? And when can a team send large numbers of players forward and position them exactly where they wish other than at a set play? Set plays used to be regarded merely as a means of restarting the game. They should now be regarded as a means of winning it.

Set plays are obvious occasions for playing the percentages. In this chapter we shall examine the types of plays; that is the types of service and arrangements of players, which are likely to produce the best results. One point, however, should be made absolutely clear: there are some coaches and managers who are obsessed with variety at set plays. In the main these people succeed only in varying the play from something which succeeds to something which fails. Variety is important, but it needs to be variety upon a theme which is known to pay high dividends.

Free kicks

General advice is that the less complicated the play the greater the likelihood of success.

The most dangerous position for a free kick outside the penalty area is in the 'D'.

A useful strategy, if the free kick is in the 'D', is for the attackers to complete the wall thus blocking the goalkeeper's view. The ball can then be chipped over or driven through the attacker's wall which will move to let the ball through. It is important to note that the attacker's wall (see diagram 91) is placed less than ten yards from the ball. The whole of the goal is not blocked, a space is left for a direct shot past the outside of the attacker's wall.

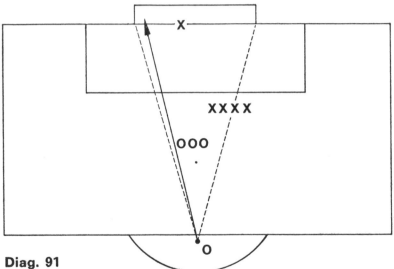

Diag. 91

One learns from watching the Brazilians that whenever they have a free kick which offers a good scoring possibility with a direct shot at goal, then they settle for the direct shot. It is also a fact that they invariably nominate a player to take these kicks who is particularly good at swerving the ball.

Many free kicks, however, are awarded in flank positions from which a direct shot at goal is not a serious proposition. These are free kicks, therefore, which require a service of the ball.

There are two major considerations for serving the ball in from the flanks:—

(1) Play the ball into the space behind the defence.
(2) Hit the ball with swerve and spin towards the goal.

If the ball is played into the space behind the defence it means that a defender must turn and play the ball whilst moving towards his goal.

If the ball is hit with spin and swerve towards the goal, it will greatly simplify the task of the attacking players in keeping the ball down.

The difficulty for forward players making contact with an out-swerve and away spin ball is to keep it down. As most cricketers know very well, if you strike against the spin the ball is likely to go up.

If players strike with the spin and with the swerve the ball is likely to go down, which is the most difficult ball for the goalkeeper to save.

Here then is a case for right-footed players taking free-kicks from the left-hand side and left-footed players taking free-kicks from the right-hand side.

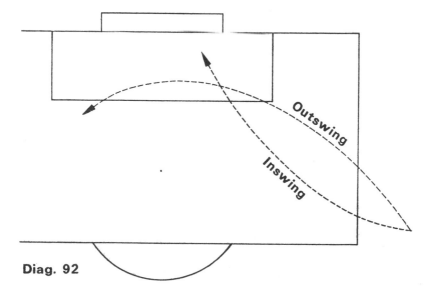

Diag. 92

Aston Villa's Gordon Cowans scores from a direct free-kick.

It is important that all the attacking players should play their part in this kick. If possible every defending player in the penalty area should be marked, by an attacker. This, one appreciates, sounds wrong. But the reasoning is this. The task of a defender is fourfold :—

(a) To keep goal-side of his immediate opponent.

(b) To keep the ball in view.

(c) To keep his immediate opponent in view.

(d) To be first to the ball.

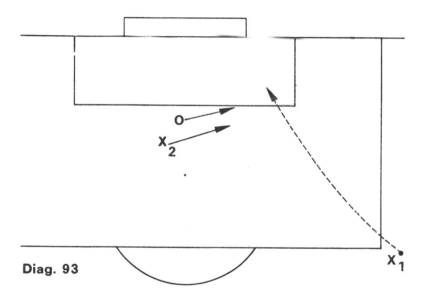

Diag. 93

In diagram 93 O is on the goal-side of X_2, and he is also in a position to keep both the ball and X_2 in view. He is also in such a position as should ensure that he is first to the ball.

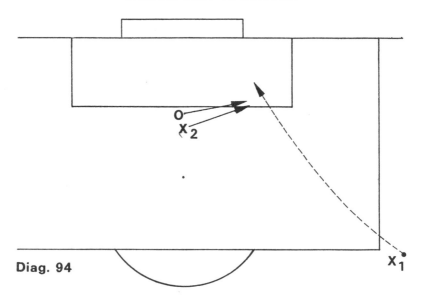

Diag. 94

In diagram 94, X_2 has moved into a position very close to O.O is still on the goal-side of X_2 and he is also in a position to keep the ball and X_2 in view. He is, however, by no means certain to be first to the ball. X_2 has everything going for him. The ball will be played into the space beyond X_2 and O so that they are running towards the goal to make a contact with the ball. Whichever player reaches the ball first will have to play with the spin because the ball is spinning away from them. For the same reason, on contact the ball will go down, not up. Under the pressure of close challenge O could easily misdirect the ball into his own goal. X_2 is in the position where he has all to gain and nothing to lose.

Under match conditions, there will be not one defender, but six or seven defenders in the penalty area plus two or three in the wall.

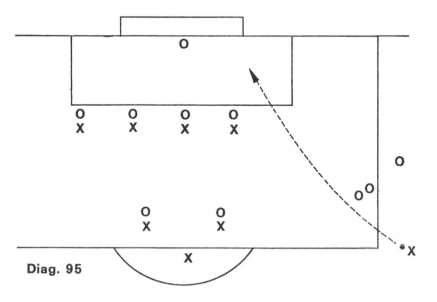

Diag. 95

Diagram 95 shows the position as it could well be in a match. It is a mistake, but quite normal, for defences to leave the near post area open. This really is an open invitation for the in spinning kick into that area. Notice that all the X players are marking their opponents and trying to get a half-yard start on them. Provided the service is accurate, and particularly where it is possible to aim for the front half of the goal ; and provided attackers mark defenders, then this type of free kick represents one's best chance of scoring from flank positions around the penalty area.

It is also worth noting that it is in the flank areas where most free kicks are awarded and the least productive area for free kicks is the 'D'. One is wise to play the percentages in this respect also, and more time should be devoted to practising flank free kicks than free kicks directly in front of goal.

117

Taking advantage of players in the wall

The main advantage to the attacking team of having defending players in the wall is that they cannot mark players.

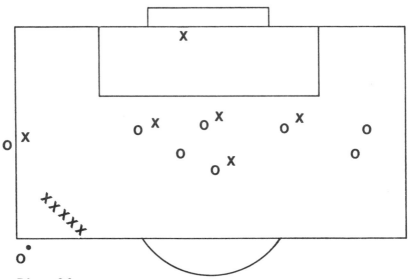

Diag. 96

In diagram 96, the X team has placed five players in the wall. This means that, excluding the goalkeeper, the X team has only five players to defend both the outside and the inside of the wall. The O team has done the correct tactical thing and produced an enormous numerical advantage in a most vital area of the field, i.e. on the inside of the wall. The position in fact is 7 O v 4 X, an equation which should equal one goal.

Attacking players should think positively and be quick to embarrass defences who lock up several players in the wall.

Free kicks in the defending half of the field

Free kicks in the defending part of the field should be taken as quickly as possible to take advantage of the breakdown in concentration which often accompanies a stoppage. The ball should also be played forward in order to put as many opponents out of the game as possible.

Free kicks in the region of the half-way line

Free kicks from the half-way line or from just inside the opponent's half of the field can be particularly dangerous. It is important at these free kicks to follow the principle of marking opponents particularly those opponents, usually four or five of them, who will form a line somewhere in the region of the edge of the penalty area. Each defender should be marked from in front, not the side, so that the ball which is delivered to them can be flipped on with a header into the space at the back of the defence.

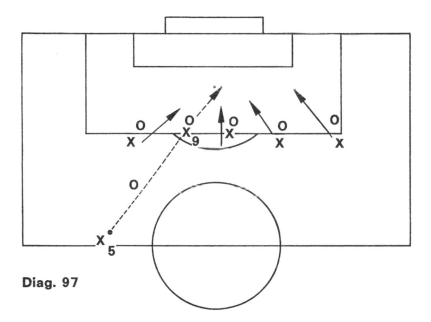

Diag. 97

In diagram 97 X_5 has played the ball to X_9 who has headed the ball on to the back of the defence. The other four X players in forward positions attack the space behind the defence as X_9 heads the ball.

Defenders in this type of position usually decide to hold the attackers to a particular line. In so doing they position themselves square across the field. In doing this they give the attackers a chance to expose all five defenders with one play. This again is a good percentage play for the attacking team.

It will be appreciated that free kicks are dangerous in almost any part of the field. When more and more teams become adept at scoring from free kicks the game will take a turn for the better, since teams will be punished in terms of results, for foul play. We should all encourage referees to use their most stringent endeavours to hasten that day.

CORNER KICKS

Modern tactics and techniques of corner kicking have established corners as a very good source of goals. Corners fall into two main categories :—
(1) Short corners.
(2) Long corners.

(1) Short corners

The advantage of the short corner is to take the kick quickly and produce a two against one or three against two situation in the area of the corner, thus providing the opportunity to move into a much more dangerous position nearer to goal and at a better angle.

It is important that players who move out to the corner to support the short kick should try and move into the danger area to join the action once the kick is taken.

(2) Long corners

Long corners fall into two categories—in-swing and out-swing. As with free kicks the same principle applies—in-swerve and in-spin assists the attackers and out-swerve and out-spin makes the defender's task a little easier.

The in-swing corner

The in-swing corner is by far the most dangerous method of taking corners provided the service is accurate. The ideal area for the server to aim for is the front half of the goal just underneath the crossbar. (Diagram 98).

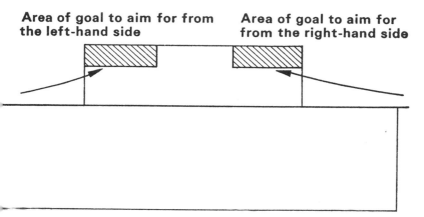

Area of goal to aim for from the left-hand side

Area of goal to aim for from the right-hand side

Diag. 98

The team organisation must support the kick and it is essential (diagram 99) that a tall player should be positioned at the near post in position (1) and a second player at position (2) on the goal-line. The player (3) has moved into his position not only to attract defenders away from central positions but also to flick the ball on should the kick be short. Players (4) and (5) attack the back-half of the goal which is where the ball is likely to arrive if it is flicked on. Players (6) and (7) position on the edge of the penalty area for the ball knocked down, or an attempted clearance.

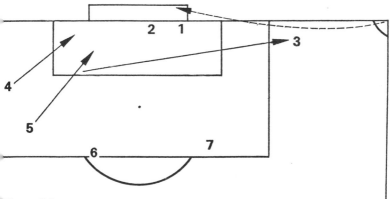

Diag. 99

121

In-swinging corners to the far post are less dangerous, generally speaking, than in-swinging corners to the near post, for the principal reason, that the ball is longer in flight and gives the defence a little more time to effect a challenge.

The out-swing corner

For reasons that have already been explained, the out-swing corner is less dangerous than the in-swing corner. Furthermore, the greater the distance the ball swings out from goal, the less dangerous the situation becomes.

Positive thinking

It is important that teams should not be nervous of sending eight players forward into the attacking area of the field for corner kicks. Positive situations call for positive action. Attackers must realise, however, that the slightest infringement will be penalised and the initiative lost.

THE THROW-IN

The danger from a throw-in is underestimated, and more players seem to relax their concentration at throws than at any other situation. Key factors to remember are as follows:—

(a) **Take the throw quickly.** If the throw is taken quickly it is the more likely that advantage can be taken of any opposing player who loses his concentration and fails to do his defensive work.

(b) **Throw to an un-marked player.** If there is an attacking player un-marked at a throw in, then there is little doubt that he will be the best player to receive the ball. Since he is un-marked he will not be pressurised and should, therefore, be in a good position to attack the opposition.

(c) **Throw the ball forward.** Unless the ball is thrown backwards to a player who is un-marked the ball should be thrown forward. In this way more defending players find themselves in positions which are on the wrong side of the ball.

(d) **Throw for easy control.** Many players who throw the ball in are careless and they do not pay sufficient attention to the quality of their throw. They should make a throw which gives the player receiving the ball the easiest possible control. If the throw is intended for the player to head the ball back to the thrower, the ball should be aimed at chest height, not head height, since this will enable the player to move easily towards the ball and head the ball through the top half, thus ensuring that the ball is returned to the thrower's feet.

(e) **Create sufficient space to make the throw effective.** One of the big mistakes at a throw-in is for the players to stand too close to the thrower. This is particularly the case in schoolboy football. As a rough guide, players should aim to position approximately 15 to 20 yards distant from the throw. If this distance is achieved, and there is no reason why it should not be, opponents will find it difficult to mark players and support each other. Furthermore, it will give the attacking players space in which to work and, if necessary, space in which to draw one's opponent close to the thrower in order to exploit the space behind him by throwing the ball over the head of the defender.

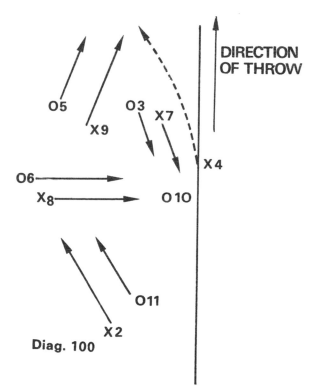

DIRECTION OF THROW

Diag. 100

In diagram 100 X_4 is taking the throw and X_7, X_9, X_8 and X_2 all position 15 to 20 yards distant from the throw. As X_4 prepares to throw the ball X_7, marked by O_3, and X_8, marked by O_6, move towards the throw thus creating space behind them. X_9 moves into the space created by X_7 and X_2 moves into the space created by X_8. This is a very simple but effective play. Were it not simple, of course, it would not work. But the players need practice in order to time their runs correctly.

(f) **Try and get the thrower back in the game.** Very often the player throwing the ball in loses his concentration when he has thrown the ball. In consequence he goes out of the game for a few seconds and allows the opposition to gain a numerical advantage in the area of the ball. The thrower must concentrate upon getting into the action once he has thrown the ball. By so doing he can often help to establish a numerical advantage for the attacking players in the area of the ball.

The long throw

The long throw is particularly dangerous when it is executed in the attacking third of the field, and especially when it is aimed at the area of the near post.

A major requirement is a tall player to receive the ball in the near post area. A second requirement is good support team organisation to attack the spaces into which the ball may be played.

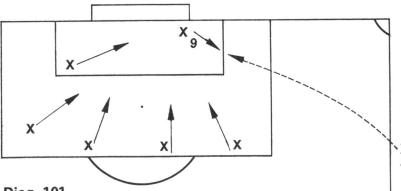

Diag. 101

Diagram 101 shows X_9 receiving a long throw from X_4 and the other five X players providing 'round the clock' support for X_9. It is important that X_4, having thrown the ball, should follow in support of his throw.

The long throw is yet another example of the importance of sending large numbers of players forward to give full support in the most positive manner possible.

CONCLUSION AND SUMMARY

All set plays are potentially dangerous. Success depends on three factors :—

(1) Good team planning and organisation to get the best out of the players as individuals and as a team.

(2) A disciplined performance by the players.

(3) An accurate service of the ball.

In the end everything stands or falls on the accuracy of the service. There is just one word of advice for those who are not sufficiently accurate . . . practice ! Try and remember the following points :—

(1) 40% of goals are scored from set plays.

(2) Free kicks :—
   (a) The less complicated the better.
   (b) Go for direct shots in front of goal.
   (c) In-swinging and in-spinning balls are more dangerous than out-swinging and away spinning balls.
   (d) It is important for attackers to 'mark' defenders and be first to the ball.
   (e) Do not be afraid to send large numbers of players forward into attacking positions.
   (f) Take free kicks in the defending part of the field quickly to take advantage of the breakdown in the concentration of opponents.

(3) Corner kicks :—
   (a) The advantage of the short corner—numerical advantage.
   (b) The importance of the in-swing corner into the front half of the goal.
   (c) The importance of the team organisation to support the kick—positive thinking.

(4) Throw in :—
   (a) Take the throw quickly.
   (b) Throw to an un-marked player.
   (c) Throw the ball forward.
   (d) Throw for easy control.
   (e) Create sufficient space to make the throw effective.
   (f) Try and get the thrower back in the game.
   (g) The long throw—good support team organisation.

CHAPTER 12

GOALKEEPING

A goalkeeper has five main areas of responsibility, the fifth of which is responsibility for defending at set plays. We have dealt with this facet in Chapter Ten.

The remaining four areas of responsibility which we shall deal with in this chapter are :—

(1) Dealing with shots.

(2) Dealing with crosses.

(3) Supporting the defence.

(4) Distribution.

(1) Stopping shots—holding the ball and knocking the ball away

The first objective for a goalkeeper in relation to shot stopping is to understand that a goalkeeper either holds shots or he knocks them away to safety. Losing possession without clearing the ball is the number one cardinal sin of goalkeeping. In order to be sure of holding the ball a goalkeeper should endeavour to get his body behind the ball. In order to clear the ball the goalkeeper requires to apply force to the ball. The quicker the goalkeeper makes up his mind whether he can hold the ball or whether he should clear the ball the more efficient he will be.

Narrowing the angle

A goalkeeper should understand that his best chance of stopping shots is to reduce the amount of goal which his opponent has to aim at. Even by moving a yard or two off his goal-line the goal-keeper will reduce the amount of space for the attacker to shoot into.

West Bromwich Albion's Bryan Robson shoots past Valencia goalkeeper, Manzadedo, but the ball went wide of the goal.

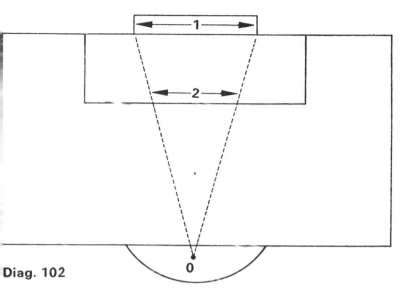

Diag. 102

In diagram 102 the goalkeeper is shown in position (1) on his goal-line. In this position the maximum amount of goal is exposed and, therefore, the task of the goalkeeper in stopping shots is at its most difficult. In position (2) which is five yards out from goal, much less of the goal is exposed and, therefore, the task of the goalkeeper is made a little easier. Of course, a goalkeeper must not come too far out of his goal, otherwise the ball is likely to be played over his head. But if the ball is outside the penalty area the goalkeeper is taking little risk in moving four or five yards off his line. Obviously, the greater the reach of a goalkeeper the less likely he is to be beaten by a lob.

Goalkeeper against a forward clear of the defence

Sometimes a goalkeeper will find himself in the position where the defence is completely beaten and an opponent with the ball has a clear run at goal.

The goalkeeper must now narrow the angle still further.

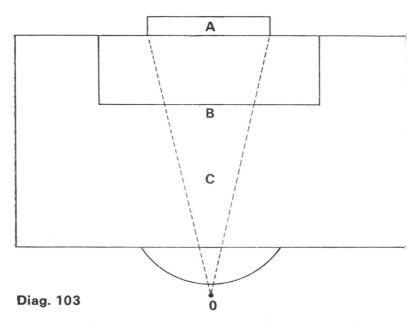

Diag. 103

Diagram 103 shows that the goalkeeper's chances are better at point C than they are at point B: and his chances are better at point B than they are at point A.

In moving out from goal, the goalkeeper should observe three important points :—

(a) Move out quickly but under control

The time for a goalkeeper to move quickly is whilst the ball is outside the playing distance of the attacking player. Once the attacking player is within playing distance of the ball, i.e. when it is conceivable that the attacker could shoot at any moment, then the goalkeeper should move with much more caution and ensure that he is sufficiently well-balanced to be able to move quickly to any shot played to either side of him. If the goalkeeper is moving very quickly in a forward direction, at the moment the shot is taken, it will be impossible for him to make a lateral movement to stop the ball.

(b) Stand up—do not dive in anticipation of the shot

Just as it was seen in Chapter Three that it is essential for defenders to stay on their feet and avoid 'selling' themselves, so the same principle applies to the goalkeeper. Once the goalkeeper goes to ground he is finished—he is totally committed and out of the game.

Goalkeepers should understand that it is a mistake of the first order to dive in anticipation of a shot. Make the attacker make the first move.

(c) Present your body as a long barrier when you go down

The barrier should be across the angle of the triangle formed by the lines joining the three points of the two posts and the ball.

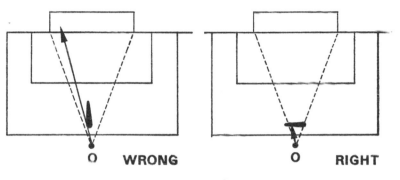

O **WRONG**	O **RIGHT**
Diag. 104	**Diag. 105**

In diagram 104 the goalkeeper has presented the narrowest possible barrier in front of his goal by diving either feet first or head first at the ball. That is wrong. In diagram 105 the goalkeeper has presented his body as a long barrier in front of his goal by spreading his body across the angle of the triangle formed by the ball and the two posts. That is good goalkeeping and is correct.

Remember, when goalkeepers present a long barrier and block the shot it is not luck, it is good goalkeeping. When goalkeepers present a narrow barrier and let the ball into the net it is not bad luck it is bad goalkeeping.

(2) Crosses—when to catch and when to punch

Nothing tests quite so well the confidence and authority of a goalkeeper as crosses. At first consideration it would appear that because the goalkeeper can use his hands, crosses should never present a problem. This is not so. There are several possible pitfalls of which a goalkeeper should be aware.

131

Liverpool's Ray Clemence leaps above Nottingham Forest's Larry Lloyd.

(a) The distance to the ball

If it is possible for a goalkeeper to reach a cross he should do so, because he should be the best player in the team to deal with that particular situation. But the goalkeeper can only deal with the situation if he can get to the ball. If the ball is too far out from goal for the goalkeeper to reach, then he should elect to stay and defend his goal.

In diagram 106 X has elected to move out from goal to intercept the cross from O_1 to O_2. X, however, has failed to reach the line of flight, misses the ball and has, therefore, left the whole of his goal exposed for O_2 to play the ball into goal.

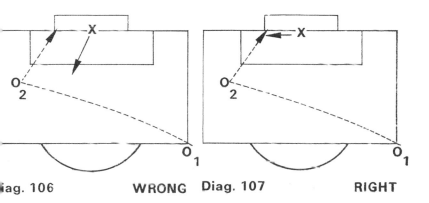

| iag. 106 | **WRONG** | Diag. 107 | **RIGHT** |

In diagram 107 X has elected to stay and defend his goal since he assessed that the distance from goal to intercept the cross was too great. As long as the goalkeeper knows what he can do and is decisive in making his decisions, he is correct. Most poor goalkeeping is the result of indecision.

(b) The ground route to the ball

The goalkeeper may assess that he can cover the distance to the ball only to find that the ground route is blocked because the area is heavily populated with players. This situation is always likely to occur from crosses from set plays when the opposition has sent up seven or eight players into the penalty area. Again the same principle applies: if there is any doubt in the goalkeeper's mind about his reaching the ball then the goalkeeper should elect to stay and defend his goal.

Nottingham Forest goalkeeper Peter Shilton dives bravely at the feet of Southampton strikers Nick Holmes and Phil Boyer.

England striker Steve Coppell (hidden behind 14) scores the winner for England past Scotland goalie Alan Rough.

(c) Challenge when catching the ball

Another serious pitfall for the goalkeeper is the challenge when he is trying to catch the ball. Sound advice for goalkeepers is to decide early whether to catch or punch the ball. If the decision is to catch the ball then the ball must be taken at the highest possible point in trajectory, thereby emphasising the advantage which a goalkeeper has over all other players.

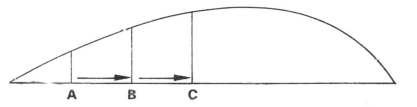

Diag. 108

In diagram 108 position A represents the standing height of the goalkeeper. Clearly, at that point in trajectory the goalkeeper stands no better chance of taking the ball than any other player.

Position B represents the height of the goalkeeper with his arms outstretched above his head. Obviously position B gives the goalkeeper some advantage over all other players, but not a clear advantage, since players who jump will still have a chance of a successful challenge for the ball.

Position C, which represents the goalkeeper's height with his arms outstretched after having jumped, is the only position in which the goalkeeper can be certain that he has a clear and decisive advantage over all other players.

Even in this position, should the goalkeeper be in doubt concerning his ability to catch the ball, possibly because of the challenge of opposing players, then he should elect to punch the ball.

(d) Punching the ball

If the decision is to punch the ball, then the goalkeeper must punch for height, distance and width in that order. It is important that the decision to punch the ball should be made early, in order that the goalkeeper will have the opportunity to exert the full power of his body momentum into the punch.

England goalkeeper Peter Shilton punches clear under pressure.

Goalkeepers are less than realistic if they expect to deal with crosses without the pressure of physical challenge. This pressure is likely to be particularly strong in the early stages of a game. A goalkeeper will more easily establish a psychological dominance over his opponents during this period if he elects to punch the ball when challenged. The goalkeeper should remember the golden rule :—

If in doubt, do not hesitate—punch the ball

(3) Supporting the defence

A goalkeeper should always position himself in relation to the position of the ball at any given time. In doing this he will achieve three objectives.

(a) The correct angle

He will always be at the correct angle should he be required to move out from goal.

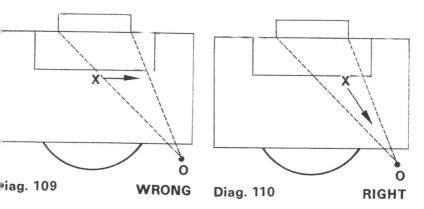

Diag. 109   **WRONG**   Diag. 110   **RIGHT**

In diagram 109 the goalkeeper, X, is at the wrong angle in relation to the position of the ball. Before X can narrow the angle he will need to move into the triangle formed by the lines joining the ball and the two posts.

In diagram 110 the goalkeeper, X, is in the correct position, being at the correct angle and in position, if necessary, to narrow the angle still further by moving out from goal.

137

(b) Support the space behind the defence

He will be in a position to support the defence—that is reduce the amount of space between the rear-most defender and the goal.

In diagram 111 the X team is pressing an attack on their opponent's goal and the ball is in the opposing penalty area. The goalkeeper has moved to the edge of the penalty area in order to decrease the amount of space between himself and his rear defenders who are on the half-way line.

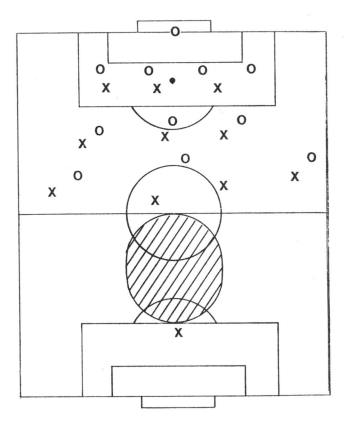

Diag. 111

TACTICS AND TEAMWORK

In this position the goalkeeper is not only physically near to his team-mates and, therefore, decreasing the space between himself and them, but he will find it much easier to shout instructions to his team-mates. Calling is a most important part of goalkeeping and is grossly underestimated by most goalkeepers. The goalkeeper, in fact, is usually in the best position to see all the movements by attackers and can often cause potential danger to be averted by calling to his team-mates.

(c) Concentration

It will ensure that the goalkeeper concentrates all the time. Loss of concentration is the great enemy of goalkeepers, particularly in games where the goalkeeper is having very few touches of the ball.

(4) Distribution

There is a vast difference between getting rid of the ball and passing the ball. The responsibility on a goalkeeper, like any other player in possession of the ball, is to pass the ball. This he will do in one of two ways :—

First by throwing the ball

Throws should not only be accurate but they should give the player receiving the ball as easy a control as possible. If the ground route to the player is clear, with no possibility of an interception, then the ball should be thrown along the ground, except in very wet or muddy conditions.

If the player receiving the ball has his back to his opponent then a call should be given to indicate whether he can turn with the ball, whether he should hold the ball, or whether he should play the ball off quickly.

Second kicking from hand

There are two types of kicks from hand :—
(a) The volley.
(b) The half-volley.
(a) **The volley** invariably has a high trajectory and travels less distance than the half-volley. It also takes longer to reach its target. As against that it is a safe kick in all ground conditions. The purpose of a long kick is not only to find players in an attacking part of the field but also to gain a territorial advantage. Particularly if the ball can be played into the opponent's half of the field there is every chance that even if an opponent gets his head to the ball the attacking players will gain secondary possession in an important part of the field.

It is important to test out defences against the long high ball and the goalkeeper must then make a judgment concerning the success or failure of this particular play in any particular match.

(b) **The half-volley** will normally travel further and reach its target quicker than a volley. It is not, however, as easy for the goalkeeper to control and on a muddy pitch the results of half-volley kicking can be disastrous. Goalkeepers would be well advised not to attempt half-volley kicks on a muddy pitch.

However, on a dry pitch and with a following wind, the ball can often be played to the back of the opposing defence to great advantage. All goalkeepers should try and develop the technique of half-volley kicking.

One further point should be made about goalkeeper's distribution at this stage. Many goalkeepers have developed the habit of rolling the ball whilst they look for a player to pass to. Unfortunately, once they see the player they wish to pass to, they have to pick the ball up before they can pass the ball. Vital seconds are lost and what was a good position before the goalkeeper picked the ball up, may not be such a good position when he actually gets around to passing the ball.

Unless a goalkeeper, therefore, is rolling the ball to the edge of the penalty area for the purpose of gaining a better territorial advantage, he is far better off standing still with the ball in his hands. His distribution from that position will be both quicker and more effective.

Goal-kicks

A goalkeeper will be responsible for taking goal-kicks. It is not a good policy for out-field players to take goal-kicks, for the good reason that by so doing one presents the opposition with a numerical advantage in the area of the field where the ball is played.

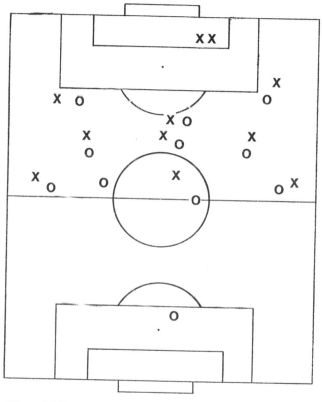

Diag. 112

Diagram 112 shows the position at a goal-kick for the X team which is being taken by an out-player. Numerically, outside the two penalty areas nine X players are playing against ten O players. Tactically, that is an unsatisfactory arrangement. If the goalkeeper is a poor kicker of the ball he must practise to improve his technique and accept his responsibility for goal-kicks.

Gaining a numerical advantage at goal-kicks

Goal-kicks should be a means of starting attacks and the goalkeeper should consider taking his kick quickly to put opponents out of the game. He must also consider the quality of his kick and the degree of ease or difficulty for his team-mate in receiving the pass.

CONCLUSION AND SUMMARY

Of all the eleven individuals in a football team the goalkeeper is the most important. If his performance is poor he can and does lose matches on his own account. If his performance is good, he gives his team-mates confidence and often inspires them to play above themselves.

Try and remember the following points:—

(1) Stopping shots:—
   (a) Hold the shot or knock it away to safety.
   (b) Narrow the angle—move under control—stand up.
   (c) When you do go down at an opponent's feet, present your body as a long barrier.

(2) Crosses:—
   (a) Distance to the ball.
   (b) Ground route to the ball.
   (c) Challenge when catching the ball.
   (d) Take the ball at the highest possible point in trajectory.
   (e) If in doubt, punch the ball.

(3) Supporting the defence:—
   (a) Be at the correct angle.
   (b) Support the space behind the defence.
   (c) Concentrate all the time and give the necessary instructions to the players in front of you.

(4) Distribution:—
   (a) Throwing—quality of service.
   (b) Kicking from hand—the advantages of the volley and the half-volley kicks.
   (c) Goal-kicks—accept responsibility—quality of service—try and gain a numerical advantage.

CHAPTER 13

FITNESS FOR ASSOCIATION FOOTBALL

It would be improper to end this book without writing a chapter on fitness. Everything that happens in the game depends on fitness and it is impossible to play at a high level without a corresponding level of fitness. Furthermore, modern strategy is making even greater demands on each player's physical power and endurance. This trend will not be reversed.

Fitness for Association Football does not only involve, however, physical fitness—it involves mental fitness also. It is impossible to determine exactly where physical fitness ends and mental fitness starts. It is also impossible to know the influence which a player's physical state has upon his mental state and the influence his mental state has upon his physical state. It can, however, be stated with certainty that there is an influence and an inter-relatedness between a player's mental and physical state. It will, therefore, be understood that it is a mistake to concentrate all fitness training on the physical aspect of fitness.

It is also a mistake to place too much reliability upon a player's performance in training. It will be within the experience of many of the readers of this book to know of players who regularly give 100% effort in training but who appear to give less than 100% in matches. Conversely there are players who appear to give less than 100% effort in training but who in matches give 100% plus. Of course, this is not a reason why all players should not be pressed to give 100% effort in training. They should. It is, however, the reason why it should be understood that in the last analysis the only reliable guide as to a player's fitness is his performance in competitive matches.

Before one can understand how to achieve fitness for football one must understand the causes and effects of fatigue in footballers.

What causes fatigue in footballers?

It is a combination of four factors:—

(1) Running.
(2) Work to overcome inertia.
(3) Physical contact.
(4) Mental concentration and tension.

TACTICS AND TEAMWORK

(1) **Running.** All running contributes towards fatigue. The running which a footballer does is of an unrhythmic nature—some of it is fast, some of moderate speed and some slow. There is some doubt as to how much running a player does in the course of 90 minutes football. An analysis of the Great Britain Olympic Team, however, in a match against Sheffield Wednesday in 1971 revealed that all the players were covering total distances of between 12,000 yards and 16,500 yards each player and approximately 25% of these distances were covered at speed. Other investigations suggest that these distances are probably correct.

Even on the top figure, however, of 16,500 yards or just over nine miles, i.e. one mile per ten minutes of the game, this is still only a moderate performance by comparison with athletic performances. The comparison, however, is not fair since there are so many other factors which contribute towards the total fatigue of a footballer.

(2) **Work to overcome inertia.** This is work to overcome the resistance of one's own body weight, i.e. stopping, starting, turning, jumping, tackling, getting up off the ground etc. The hardest thing for a footballer to do physically once he has started running, is not to continue running, but to stop and turn. If in addition a player has to run through mud or on spongy grass the physical effort required is even greater. Unrhythmic running, that is running at varying speeds, is more tiring than even-paced running. But unrhythmic running punctuated frequently by work to overcome inertia is even more tiring. This is the very type of work which a footballer has to undertake. But that is not the end of a footballer's problem as far as fatigue is concerned.

(3) **Physical contact.** Football is very much a game of physical contact. A player will tackle and be tackled; he will challenge and be challenged for the ball in heading duals. Occasionally he will collide with players and occasionally he will be struck quite painful blows with the ball. Every time a player suffers a physical contact a little more energy is sapped away. It is, perhaps, interesting to consider the physical performance of boxers. Is it the physical movement around the ring which primarily causes fatigue in boxers or is it the physical blows which they have to endure? One would not wish to encourage readers to make a comparison between football and boxing but I hope the point is established that the normal fair and reasonable physical contact which a player can expect in football is a contributory factor towards fatigue.

(4) **Mental concentration and tension.** There is no doubt that mental concentration is tiring. Anyone who has attended a meeting will appreciate the fact. The process of simply sitting around a

table for a couple of hours mainly concentrating upon what other people are saying is tiring. Driving a car for several hours is tiring. But these efforts are nothing by comparison with the footballer who constantly is required to assess each situation always trying to think ahead and outwit his opponent. And that is to say nothing of the tension which inevitably surrounds every important game and raises a player's desire and even anxiety to do well and also invokes in him a fear of failure. This undoubtedly is a cause of fatigue and may be a greater drain on a player's energy than any of us know.

It is a combination of all these factors which causes fatigue in footballers.

What are the effects of fatigue?

(1) **A decrease in work rate.** As a player gets tired he will not only undertake less work, i.e. he will cover less ground but he will also cover the ground less quickly. The moral behind this fact is that players will play when they are fatigued and they must practise when they are fatigued also since a player must learn to adjust his performance in accordance with his physical limitations and still be efficient within his limited capacity. A player who fails to adjust will attempt the impossible and be inefficient.

(2) **Decrease in powers of judgment.** As a player gets tired so his judgment begins to falter. He will see the ball less quickly and he will assess situations less quickly. It is interesting to watch people, particularly children, when they are tired—they invariably rub their eyes. Eyesight deteriorates with fatigue. This factor is likely to affect the high class player more than the low class player since he is more likely to suffer when the edge is taken off his performance.

(3) **Decrease in technical performance.** It follows almost without saying that if a player suffers a decrease in judgment he is likely to suffer a decrease in technical performance. His control of the ball is likely to be less good and his passing less accurate.

(4) **Decrease in powers of concentration.** Of course, we all know that it is more difficult to concentrate when we are tired. The efficiency of a footballer in a team performance depends very largely on his concentrating on the task he has to perform. At set play situations, for example, it is vital that every player does the job allotted to him. If one player fails the whole team is likely to fail.

This is yet another example of why players should practise when they are fatigued in order to learn how to adjust their performances in order to retain essential team efficiency.

Tension and concentration show on the faces of Pat Jennings, Brian Talbot, Steve Walford and Kenny Dalglish.

(5) **More susceptible to injury.** There is some medical opinion which suggests that a player in a fatigued state is more likely to sustain certain types of injuries chief amongst which are muscle tears.

What then is the object of training for footballers and what is the definition of fitness?

Fitness is the capacity to delay the onset of fatigue

A player, therefore, as he gets fitter becomes fatigued less quickly. It inevitably follows, therefore, that a fit player will be more efficient than an unfit player. The fundamental question is, of course, how does one delay the onset of fatigue? The answer is that players must work to achieve higher fitness levels and this they can only do by working in accordance with the principle of overload.

The principle of overload

Overload is a question of doing a little more this week or this session than one did last week or at the last session. It should be understood that a player's level of fitness is unlikely to stand still for very long. A player will either get more fit or he will become less fit. A player will not become more fit by doing the same amount of work each week. At best that will only retain a level of fitness.

It is possible to over-train. This is a state which is reached when a player attempts too much too soon. It is usually caused by either a player's enthusiasm getting the better of him or a coach or trainer failing to understand how to apply the principle of overloading.

There are five main ways in which the principle of overloading can be applied in training:—

(1) By increasing the number of repetitions of a given activity. If, for example, a player did ten fifty yard runs one could increase the load at the next session by asking the player to do eleven fifty yard runs.

(2) By increasing the speed of the repetitions. If, to continue the example, each of the fifty yard runs was done in ten seconds one could ask the player to do the runs in nine seconds.

(3) By increasing the length of each repetition. By this means one would ask the player to run sixty yards instead of fifty yards.

(4) By decreasing the rest period between each repetition. If the player had a thirty second rest between each one of his fifty yard runs one could decrease the rest period or interval to twenty-five seconds.

(5) By increasing the load. One could obviously increase the load by asking the player to wear a weighted jacket or weighted boots. One could also increase the load by asking the player to make his runs uphill. There is, however, a danger when applying this particular technique to running. The danger is that one will inadvertently invoke a different type of running to that required in the game.

The same criticism can be made against the use of spiked running shoes for footballers. These shoes, with spikes only in the soles, throw the body forward at an angle which is detrimental to footballers when they have to turn or adjust their bodies to new positions very quickly.

On balance it is better to regard increasing the load as essentially a technique for weight training in order to increase the resistance.

By the astute use, and by combining the use, of these methods of overloading, and exercising patience by progressing in small rather than large steps, a good trainer or coach will achieve outstanding results.

What, however, are the physical qualities which a footballer needs to improve? There are two main qualities :—

(1) Endurance.
(2) Strength.

(1) Endurance

It is not generally understood that there are four main types of endurance.

(a) **Static endurance.** A good example of this type of endurance would be holding an arm outstretched for as long as possible. In time the arm becomes fatigued and drops. I cannot think why anyone would wish to practise this activity and certainly static endurance has no part to play in a footballer's fitness training programme.

(b) **Rhythmic endurance.** An example of this type of endurance would be skipping. Again football is not a rhythmic game and, therefore, rhythmic endurance has nothing to commend it to footballers.

(c) **Sustained endurance.** This is the type of endurance achieved by long distance runners. There is little doubt that this type of endurance is required by footballers.

Medical science has revealed that the hearts of those who engage in sustained endurance work have a rather large chamber with relatively thin walls. It is also a fact that the resting pulse rates of those who engage in sustained endurance training are much lower than those who engage in other types of training. It is not uncommon for long distance runners to have resting pulse rates in the middle thirties.

One advantage of a low resting pulse rate is that a man will recover more quickly from a given amount of activity than the man who has a high resting pulse rate. There can be little doubt that the advantage to a footballer of having the capacity to recover quickly and frequently from short but high intensity work loads is considerable. It necessarily follows, therefore, that effective football training will involve sustained endurance work.

(d) **Power endurance.** This is the type of endurance which a sprinter requires in order to sustain his effort in the last twenty-five yards of a one hundred yard race. This also is the quality which a footballer must have to sustain and maintain the quality of his power performances punctuated, as they are, frequently throughout the game.

Players who train only for power endurance will develop thick heart walls with a relatively small chamber.

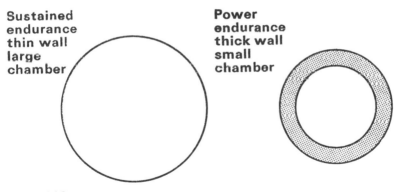

Sustained endurance thin wall large chamber

Power endurance thick wall small chamber

Diag. 113

Footballers must seek to combine both sustained and power endurance methods in order to achieve the best of both 'hearts'.

During a football match, when a player is called upon to make a maximum effort, he will incur what is known as an oxygen debt. This means that he has made his effort without taking into his body the amount of oxygen required for the activity. Nature requires, however, that he must repay that debt immediately the activity is over. During the period when a player has incurred an oxygen debt he is likely to be less efficient, because he is fatigued. The efficiency of a player, therefore, may ebb and flow during a game depending on how many times a player incurs an oxygen debt and depending on the size of the debt. The less fit the player is the greater will be the debt for a given amount of work, and the slower his recovery.

It is important to remember that the lower a player's resting pulse rate is, the more work he will be able to undertake before he incurs an oxygen debt.

It is also important to remember that the more power endurance training a player undertakes the greater his oxygen debt capacity is likely to be.

Without doubt, therefore, a footballer should train to achieve a high level of sustained endurance and also a high level of power endurance.

Sustained endurance will involve running at a sustained pace for something of the order of seven or eight miles. It should be possible for players to average a seven minute mile for seven or eight miles.

Power endurance will involve working at high intensity for periods not in excess of 35 seconds.

A popular method of training for power endurance is to do shuttle runs. These runs are usually over a distance of 150 yards and involve several turns.

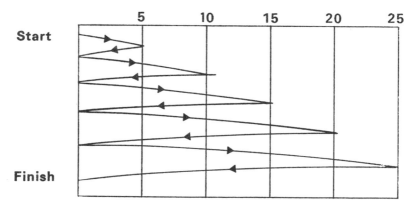

Diag. 114

To achieve the level of fitness required for football it is necessary to do rather more than 2,000 yards using this type of training.

It will be observed that the longest run in one direction in a shuttle run is 25 yards. In the game there will be many runs which are made which will be more than 25 yards. Indeed one of the interesting aspects of modern strategy is that players, particularly players moving forward from mid-field or from rear positions, are making runs of 50, 60 or even 70 yards. This needs to be taken account of in training.

The shuttle running type of run and the longer distance type of run should total in the region of 3,500-4,000 yards. The runs should also be broken up, i.e. it would be a mistake to do all the shuttle runs one after the other. This would have a tendency to produce rhythmic endurance and the player would become good at shuttle running but very little else.

It should also be observed that not only should the runs be broken up in order that the player cannot develop a rhythm but the intervals between the various intense efforts should be irregular for the same reason.

It is, of course, self-evident that distances and times should be recorded otherwise overloading is not possible.

It is also worth making the point that these types of runs which require maximum effort are better done without a ball. Physically, a player can work harder without a ball.

Provided also that players can keep their times close together, i.e. 30-35 seconds for a shuttle run, there should be no need to record a separate time for each individual player.

During intervals between intense activity it is best for players to continue working at some less exacting activity, e.g. 5 v 5 keep ball or one or two touch football, for a matter of two or three minutes only. In this way players are involved in the game in a fatigued state and have to concentrate on a specific task.

Physical contact should not be neglected in the training. One appreciates that Managers are reluctant to run the risk of having a player injured in training. Unfortunately, it is a risk which has to be taken.

A good activity is 1 v 1 for not more than 45 seconds. The players will work hard at this activity but not flat out, hence the time of 45 seconds, not 35 seconds. The best arrangements are for each player to have a goal about 20 yards apart. There should be no touch lines since the ball is in play at all times.

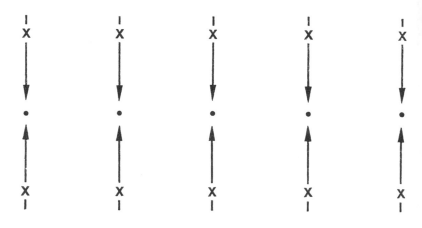

Diag. 115

Each player stands in front of his goal with the ball equidistant between them. On a blast of the whistle the players move to challenge for the ball and the activity continues for 45 seconds.

It is preferable to have a small goal otherwise players will be encouraged to shoot from long distances and the physical pressure will be relieved whilst the ball is being retrieved.

This type of activity will not only produce physical contact but will also contribute towards power endurance and work to overcome inertia.

(2) Strength

There is only one way in which to gain strength and that is by progressive resistance activities which almost invariably take the form of weight training. There is little doubt that strength is the basis of power and strength is also the basis of speed. There is also little doubt that football managers in general do not yet accept the efficacy of strength training.

Fears of players becoming muscle-bound are completely without foundation.

Weight training must be well supervised and well controlled. The activities need only be few in number but should be carefully selected. All round body strength should be the object. Clubs and players should seek the advice of a weight training expert in establishing suitable schedules. Weight training is not dangerous unless people behave in an irresponsible manner. There is literally nothing to fear in weight training and footballers have much to gain by using weights. Remember, however, whilst it is important to start with light weights it is the heavy weights with low repetitions (approximately 6-10) which alone can produce the required strength.

It is also important to understand that strength is not an enduring quality. Having gained strength, shall we say in pre-season training, there will be a loss of strength during the season if the strength training is not continued. Deterioration begins to take place after a lapse of about ten days.

There is no reason why strength training should not be done as part of a whole fitness training session. If this is done strength training should take place last of all in the session. Perhaps it is also worth stressing that the fitness training session should be the last activity in a session which players undertake. It is a mistake to ask players to undertake a fitness training session and then follow the session with tactical work or any learning situation. When players are heavily fatigued they are in no state to concentrate upon learning. Furthermore when players are fatigued and sweating they need a shower.

Assuming players can undertake two training sessions each week it would be desirable in the fitness training part of one session to concentrate upon sustained endurance training. This could very well take the form of a seven mile run to be completed in 50 minutes.

On the second day the concentration in the fitness training session should be placed upon power endurance and strength training. One would select activities from four main areas. In most activities there is an overlapping of physical qualities. For example it is not possible to undertake physical contact activities without also involving in the same activity work to overcome inertia. This fact should be appreciated when trying to assess the total affect of any one training session.

(1) **Power endurance.** In this area of activity one is thinking of the shuttle running type of activity and also the power work to overcome inertia. One will also include the longer type of runs which are made in the game. The total distance will be of the order of 3,500-4,000 yards.

(2) **Body contact.** One will select in this area activities such as 1 v 1 which ensure fair but frequent body contact.

(3) **Mental concentration.** In this area the players should be required to concentrate upon some aspect of football. An ideal way to do this is to condition a small-sided game. It is, however,

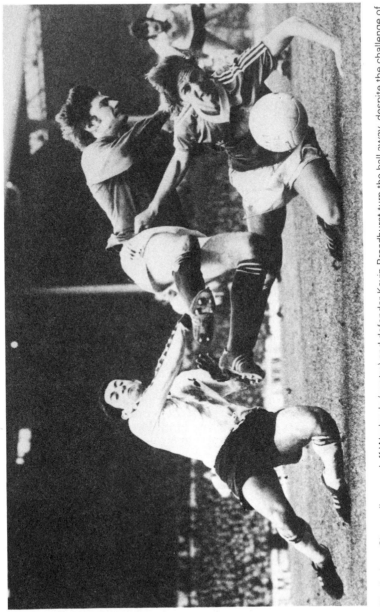

Birmingham City goalkeeper Jeff Wealands (centre) and defender Kevin Broadhurst turn the ball away, despite the challenge of Spurs' Argentinian, Osvaldo Ardiles (left).

important that the players should be required to concentrate upon a football activity rather than some other activity.

(4) **Strength.** This area of activity would best come at the end of the session. Whilst it is important and convenient that strength training should come at the end of the fitness training session the activities from the other three areas should be completely mixed in order to break up the rhythm of the session as much as possible.

The whole session should be completed in a matter of 45 minutes.

Mental Fitness

Mental fitness for football is concerned with three main areas :—

(1) Enthusiasm.
(2) Aggression.
(3) Confidence.

(1) **Enthusiasm.** This is a quality which one may describe as the self-motivator. The player who is enthusiastic is keen—he wants to participate, he wants to be involved. Enthusiasm shows itself off the field in several ways, punctuality and smartness being prime examples. On the field the enthusiastic player works hard and he wants to be involved in the play. This type of enthusiasm often rubs off on to other players. Enthusiastic players rarely cause major managerial problems.

It is difficult to give enthusiasm to the player who is deficient in that quality. If a young player lacks enthusiasm then the prognosis as far as top level performance is concerned can only be poor. Players as they get older often begin to lose the self-motivation and therefore enjoy their game less than previously. This, however, by no means applies to all players and indeed it is remarkable how many experienced players retain their boyish enthusiasm for football.

The Manager or Coach will best be able to make his players enthusiastic by himself displaying keenness. Enthusiasm is certainly infectious. Many players have got the symptoms—a much smaller number have actually got the disease—total and incurable. The prognosis for them is excellent. Never underestimate the importance of enthusiasm.

(2) **Aggression.** It is not possible to be highly competitive without the quality of aggression. There are, however, four facets of aggression which are important to the footballer.

(a) Aggression in challenging for the ball.

Football really consists of a whole series of situations where one player is competing against an opponent to defeat him. It may be sprinting to try and reach the ball first; it may be jumping to defeat an opponent in the air, it may be tackling to dispossess an opponent of the ball. In every case, however, the aggressive player realises the winner gets everything, the player who comes second gets nothing. It is this attitude, this spirit of intent which is much more important than height or weight or power or strength.

It is difficult to develop and train this quality of aggression. Certainly training should be highly competitive but most of all, players should understand that this quality is more concerned with the state of mind than with flesh and bone.

(b) Aggression within oneself.

Some players seem to have a low pain barrier and stop very easily and very quickly when they experience physical pain. One is referring here to the physical pain caused by intense physical effort—the pain of bursting lungs, leaden legs and the feeling of utter sickness.

The player with aggression within himself can force himself through these pain barriers. His mind, his singlemindedness of purpose overcomes all adversities.

Again this is primarily an attitude of mind. It can be improved by training. Players who experience the intense physical pain of intense effort for the first time are frequently afraid. It is the fear of something dreadful happening to them, rather than the actual pain, which defeats many players. If players are never subjected to intense physical effort, and the resultant pain, in training, then they are unlikely to overcome the barrier when they meet it in matches. Furthermore, it is easier for players to break through the barrier in training when several players will experience a similar feeling at a similar point in time. In these circumstances very often the hardest thing to do is stop. Once a player has overcome this basic fear in training there is no reason why he should not do the same in matches.

(c) Aggression in passing the ball.

There are some players who never really think about passing the ball, they only think in terms of passing the responsibility.

The aggressive passer of the ball is the player who is looking constantly for opportunities of placing opponents in positions of severe disadvantage. This type of player will always pass the ball forward if he has the opportunity to do so. His attitude to the passing of the ball is positive.

This quality can be trained. Obviously the better a player's technique the more likely he is to be aggressive in his passing. There are players who show a high degree of aggression in winning the ball and then display a lack of aggression in their passing.

It is, however, not entirely a matter of technique. Players need to be educated in their passing to know in which areas of the field they should calculate on the side of safety and in which areas to calculate on the side of risk. When players are educated in this way they balance aggression and responsibility.

(d) Aggression in taking chances and scoring goals.

There are no unselfish finishers—only bad ones. The responsibility on a player who is in a position to score a goal is to accept his responsibility and go for goal. Too often players are given credit for being unselfish when in fact they have lacked both aggression and responsibility. This quality of aggressive finishing can be trained. Indeed it is the one quality which will give a big dividend for an investment of time. Players should be educated to play the percentages in shooting. Players who never shoot never miss. That is a fact. It is also a fact that their percentage success is nil. Good goal scorers want to shoot so much that the fear of missing is not acceptable.

(3) **Confidence.** The ultimate in confidence is knowing what is required and knowing also that one can meet those requirements. That is the confidence of the real professional and there is no mistaking it when one sees it. Confidence produces composure and authority. But, like aggression, confidence in footballers is not one factor but rather a combination of several factors.

(a) Confidence in meeting physical challenge

The opposite state of mind from confidence is fear. Many players are afraid of physical challenge. Small boys very often are afraid of big boys. To put the issue in crude terms many players are afraid of being kicked out of the game. These players are afraid that their skills will disintegrate under the pressure of physical challenge. Players, however, must come to terms with the fact that Association Football is a physical contact game and that an essential part of the skill of playing is to perform skills whilst withstanding the force of physical contact. To think in terms of playing football without physical contact is as unrealistic as thinking in terms of playing without running. Players should be subjected to this physical contact in training. If this is not so, then they are training for a game which they will never play—a non-contact game. Referees too have an important part to play since they must ensure that fair physical challenge does not degenerate into intimidation. If this is allowed to happen then players will literally be kicked out of the game and the game as a game of skill is finished.

(b) Confidence in meeting the physical challenge of speed, strength and endurance

Just as there is a fear in the minds of some players that they are likely to get kicked out of the game so there is a fear in the minds of others that they are likely to get run off their feet. This fear is born of doubts concerning their own fitness. When a player really is 100% fit he never doubts that he can stay the course. He never thinks twice about whether he should chase this player or that pass. No player in World football stands out as a better example of this quality than Alan Ball. His performance for England in the World Cup Series of 1966, in terms of his confidence in his speed, strength and endurance to overcome all opponents was remarkable. But this quality is not only physical. Indeed in squeezing out the last vital ounce of effort it is entirely mental. At this stage the mind must force the body to continue when the body reactions to fatigue and pain may persuade the player to stop.

This quality then is the confidence of a player who not only knows that he is 100% fit but who also knows that he has the mental toughness to exploit that asset to the full.

(c) Confidence in one's ability to perform one's allotted task

Players may not always know what they are good at. Invariably, however, players know what they are bad at. Players may not always know which is their best position but they know the positions and the areas of the field where they feel uncomfortable. A player who is selected to play in a position or given a task to perform in which he does not feel comfortable will lack confidence and therefore, will not perform well.

The first task of a Manager or Coach is to get the best out of each player as an individual. That means that for as much of the game as possible each player should be performing the skills he is best at in the areas of the field in which he feels most comfortable. It goes almost without saying that a Manager or Coach who fails to get the best out of the players as individuals has no chance of getting the best out of the players as a team. When players are selected for a particular position, and when they are given instructions in the specific tasks they have to perform, they should feel that the job has been absolutely tailor-made for them. If this is so then they will approach their task in a mental state of maximum confidence.

(d) Confidence that the team method represents the best chance of winning

Players must believe as a team that the manner in which they are going to play represents their best chance of winning. If this is not so, then the team will not only play with less confidence but the way is clear for recrimination if a result is not achieved.

To get the best out of players as a team their assets must be co-ordinated. Teams need to be agreed upon how that is going to be done because that determines the method. It is important that players should understand what is required and why it is required. Without understanding there can be no agreement. Where there is full understanding and total agreement team confidence will be at its highest and a positive attitude will result.

Principles of training

There are five principles of training which it is helpful to remember and which will serve as a useful guide when drawing up training sessions and training programmes.

(1) **Overload.** In order to advance one's state of fitness it is necessary to attempt to do more work—hence the principle of overload. It necessarily follows, of course, that if one never overloads then it is not possible to advance one's level of fitness.

(2) **Test and measure.** If it is necessary to overload then it is necessary to know what one is overloading and by how much. Time and distances and weights are all important in achieving this principle.

(3) **Specificity.** To get the best results the movements involved in training should be as near as possible to those involved in the game. If this is not so then one is training for a different event. The man who trains hard in a swimming bath is fit for swimming but not for football.

(4) **Competition.** There must be competition. The whole game is concerned with challenge and winning and losing. For footballers competition should be such a part of training that it becomes a way of life.

(5) **Variety.** Anything repeated for too long will become tedious and even boring. At the same time change for the sake of change can be irritating. There should be sufficient variety in training to keep the players' minds alert but not so much that it becomes simply a variety act.

These principles are intended as guide-lines for those who are planning training programmes for footballers. Indeed the purpose of this chapter is simply to make trainers and coaches aware of causes and effects of fatigue and highlight certain priorities and principles of training. It is a basis for logical thinking in relation to fitness training, a basis too from which to work out a balanced training programme.

CONCLUSION

Fitness is an integral part of tactics and teamwork. If players cannot run they cannot play. A player will find it impossible to train to a standard beyond that which he believes to be possible. A Coach will find it impossible to train a player to a standard beyond that which the player believes to be necessary.

In the end everything comes down to what one believes to be necessary and what one believes to be possible. It is a question of judgment. The best tacticians, however, are the realists who calculate everything in terms of percentages and who leave as little as possible to chance. That is what winning in Association Football is about. Needless to say that is what effective tactics and effective teamwork is also about.